CALIFORNIA BIOGRAPHICAL DICTIONARY

Leland Stanford

CALIFORNIA BIOGRAPHICAL DICTIONARY

PEOPLE OF ALL TIMES AND ALL PLACES
WHO HAVE BEEN IMPORTANT TO THE HISTORY
AND LIFE OF THE STATE

American Historical Publications, Inc.
725 Market Street
Wilmington, Delaware 19801

A

•**ADAMS, EDIE** , (1929-) - entertainer, was born on April 16 in Kingston, Pennsylvania, the daughter of Sheldon Alanzo Enke and Ada Dorothy Adams. The family lived in Kingston until she was six, and then moved to Grove City, Pennsylvania and remained there for several years. They moved again to New York and stayed for one year, then to Tenafly, New Jersey where the family took roots.   After completing high school in Tenafly she studied at Julliard School of Music for five years. When she left Julliard, her intention had been to become a music teacher but that changed when she tried out as a contestant on Arthur Godfrey's "Talent Scouts." She selected a song learned at Julliard, and when musical director Archie Blyer took one look at her, he advised that she sing a pop song. Just as Blyer had predicted, she lost the contest but received job offers from nightclubs. She accepted one from a club in Toronto, Canada, and her professional career was launched.

Although she devoted several years to studying for a classical music career, when she began as a professional the breaks came quickly. She was voted Miss New York Television and Miss United States Television in quick succession, and she won the role of Eileen in the Broadway production of *Wonderful Town* over 300 competitors. She began to tour the country doing everything from stand-up comedy to high drama, in addition to singing. The Broadway production of *Wonderful Town* firmly established Edie as a name performer and she was in great demand for appearances in nightclubs and on television. She became a regular on Ernie Kovacs' CBS-TV show until she was signed to star in her second Broadway show as Daisy Mae in the musical version of Al Capp's *Lil Abner*. While appearing in the hit musical at night, Edie spent her days studying with the repected acting coach Lee Strassberg at the famed Actor's

Studio. She also took lessons in dress design at the Traphagen School of Fashion Design three evenings a week. She married Kovac and they soon moved to Los Angeles, where Edie continued to make guest appearances on television and supper clubs.

In 1960 she was signed by producer-director Billy Wilder for her first dramatic role in a motion picture. She appeared as Fred MacMurray's secretary in *The Apartment*, which also starred Jack Lemmon and Shirley Maclaine. She followed *The Apartment* with a co-starring role with Doris Day and Rock Hudson in *Lover Come Back* in which she returned to comedy. The films in which she has appeared include: *Anyone for Venice...? The Oscar, Made in Paris, It's a Mad, Mad, Mad, Mad, World, Under the Yum, Yum Tree* and *Call Me Bwana*.

Edie has embarked on several significant business ventures in recent years, including sponsorship of a chain of beauty salons and as owner and manager of an almond ranch in Bakersfield, California. As a result of the latter involvement, she has become the spokesperson for Sun Giant Almonds, the company through which she markets her yearly crop. She has also started a high fashion dress designing and manufacturing business.She made her opera debut singing the lead role in Offenback's *La Perichole* with the Seattle Opera in 1972. She married Marty Mills in 1964. After they were divorced in 1972, she married Pete Candoli.

•ADAMS, HARRIET CHALMERS, (1875-1937) - author, was born in Stockton, and later became an international traveler. Along with her husband, Franklin Pierce Adams, also of Stockton, she visited and wrote about every country which had ever been under Spanish or Portuguese rule. Some of the areas she visited were primitive and had never been seen before by a white woman. When she wasn't traveling, Adams lectured nationwide and published frequently in the *National Geographic*.

•ALEMANY, JOSEPH SADOC, (1814-1888) - archbishop of San Francisco, was born in Vich, Spain. Eight years after entering the order of Dominican monks in 1829, he was ordained as a

Roman Catholic priest and made an assistant in a school for novices in Viterleo, Italy. Alemany was named assistant pastor of the Chuch of Minerva in 1839 and was moved to Rome. His stay there was brief, however. Within two years, he was sent to America to do missionary work in Tennessee. He remained in Memphis and Nashville for the next six years, before being named provincial of the Ohio Dominicans. In 1850, he was named bishop of Monterey. The appointment came while Alemany was in Italy for a gathering of his Dominican order. Consecrated in the Church of San Carlo while there, he was soon on his way to the west coast of America. As head of the Monterey diocese, Alemany was active in establishing several schools in the state. Three years after the appointment, he was again promoted, this time he was named the first archbishop of the recently created archdiocese of San Francisco, a post he held for thirty-one years. In 1834, he stepped down as archibishop and returned to his native Spain. He is the author of the "Life of Saint Dominick." He died in Valencia, Spain.

•**ALLEN, JOHN JOSEPH, JR.**, (1899-) - U.S. congressman from California, was born in Oakland, California, and attended public schools. While a student in college, he enlisted during the First World War in the United States Navy and served as an aprrentice seaman. He graduated from the University of California, Berkeley, in 1920, and from its law department in 1922. Admitted to the bar in 1922, he began practicing law in Oakland. From 1923 to 1943, he was a member of the Oakland Board of Education and served several terms as its president. In addition, he was president of the California State School Trustees Association (1936-1938) and a member of the Alameda County Republican Central Committee (1936-1944). During World War Two, he served from 1942 to 1945 as a lieutenant commander in the United States Navy. After the war, he became vice chairman of the state commission on school districts in 1946 and 1947. In 1946, he was also elected as a Republican to the Eightieth Congress. Reelected five times, he was finally defeated in 1958 for a seventh term. The following year, he was appointed Under Secretary of Commerce for Transportation, a post he retained until 1961. Retired, he now lives in McCall Idaho.

•ALVARADO, JUAN BAUTISTA, (1800-1882) - the twelfth Mexican governor of California (1836-1842). He took the seat during a period of revolutionary struggles for the governorship in Monterey, after the death of Governor Figueroa, and the tumultuous, short-lived terms of Jose Castro, Nicolas Gutierrez and Mariano Chico. *Californios* favoring Alvarado's wish for a "free and soverign state' apart from the centralized government of Mexico supported him, and with the aid of 30 rifflemen, he seized control of Monterey, the capital at that time. In 1836, he was made provisional governor by the Mexican government.

Although the Mexican government had also relocated the capitol to Los Angeles at that time, Alvarado ignored the ruling and stayed in Monterey. Angry southerners caused Mexico to name another native California, Carlos Carrillo, governor in 1837, but after more conflict between the regions of the "state, "Alvarado was reappointed governor--this time officially--and the northern hero chose a subgovernor for the south, with Los Angeles as the capital. One of the Alvarado's biggest concerns as governor was for the Indians and what he saw as their oppression under the missionaries. In his opinion, the missionaries had "found the Indians in full enjoyment of their five senses, valiant in war...far-sighted in their own way; "but after the padres had left, "they left the Indian population half-stupified, very much reduced in numbers and duller...Alvarado wanted to dispose of the mission lands and secure them for land grants to political followers, which led to opposition from the missionaries.

•ANDERSON, GLENN MALCOLM, (1913-) - U.S. congressman from California, was born in Hawthorne, California, and graduated from the University of California with a B.A. in political science and psychology. He served in the U.S. Army during World War Two. In 1940, he was elected mayor of Hawthorne at the age of twenty-seven. Two years later, he was elected to the California State Assembly, where he remained until 1948. He was elected Lieutenant Governor of California in 1952 and was reelected four years later. From 1959 to 1967, he was chairman of the States Lands Commission, and from 1961 to 1967, he was a member of the Board of Trustees of California State Colleges.

Elected for the first time to Congress in 1969, Anderson has served continuously from the 91st through the 97th Congress. He was reelected to the 98th Congress in 1982.

•ANDERSON, JOHN ZUINGLIUS, (1904-) - U.S. congressman from California, was born in Oakland, California, and was reared in Santa Cruz and San Jose. Graduating from San Jose High School in 1923, he moved to San Juan Bautista in San Benito County, California, two years later and became engaged in agricultural pursuits. In 1938, he was elected as a Republican to the Seventy-sixth Congress. Reelected six times, he was not a candidate in 1952 and stepped down from office at the beginning of 1953. Later, he was a member of the board of directors of Bank of America and president of both the California Canning Pear Association and Pacific States Canning Pear Association. In 1954 and 1955, he worked with the Department of Agriculture, and then in 1956, he became an administrative assistant to President Eisenhower. When Eisenhower left office, Anderson joined the staff of the Veterans Affairs Committee of the U.S. House of Representatives. He has since retired.

•ANDREWS, LAWRENCE JAMES, (1920-) - educator and chemist, was born in San Diego, California, to Elmer J. and Florence Brown Andrews. He received his B.S. in chemistry from the University of California at Berkeley and his M.A. and Ph.D from the University of California at Los Angeles. Before joining the staff of the University of California, Davis, in 1945, he served as a lecturer at UCLA and was a research chemist with the Tennessee Eastman Corporation in Oak Ridge, Tennessee. At Davis, he was made professor of chemistry, and then chairman of the Chemistry department from 1959 to 1962. In 1964, he was promoted to Dean of the College of Letters and Sciences. During 1953-54, he was on sabbatical leave as a Ford Foundation Fellow of the Fund for the Advancement of Education. He is the author of numerous technical papers, and wrote a book with Raymond M. Keefer in 1964 entitled, *Molecular Complexes in Organic Chemistry.* He is married to Elizabeth Merriam Heggelund.

•**ANZA, JUAN BAUTISTA DE,** (1735-?) - explorer, was born in Fronteras, Sonora, Mexico. He joined the Spanish army while a youth, and rose to the rank of captain in the early 1760s. In 1774, he lead a garrison of Spanish soldiers from the Presidio of Tubac on an overland route to California, which took him through the San Jacinto mountains to the San Gabriel mission, and eventually, on to Monterey. He remained at the Monterey mission until spring, when he returned to Tubac, and was brevetted a lieutenant-colonel. The next year, he lead a another exploration to California. This time, however, the soldiers' families accompanied them, as Spain set out to colonize the San Francisco Bay area. After arriving in Monterey, where the main body of the 240-member expedition was left behind, Anza took a small party with him to San Francisco to find a location for the settlement. Anza explored the bay and around the San Joaquin River before returning to the Monterey a month later with the news that a site had been found near what is now the Golden Gate. Although he had returned to Mexico before the site was settled, he is considered the founder of San Francisco. Anza became governor of New Mexico in 1777. He remained in that position until 1788.

•**ATHERTON, GERTRUDE (FRANKLIN HORN),** (1857-1948) - author, was reared in San Francisco by her mother and her grandfather, a great grand-nephew of Benjamin Franklin. She attended private schools in both California and Kentucky, and later became a novelist, using subject matter from her own state. In 1876 she married George H. Bowen Atherton and had two children. She recalls the marriage in her *Adventures of a Novelist*, along with the story of how her husband died at sea and was returned home to her preserved in a barrel of rum.

Experiences such as these as well as her life as an independent woman filled her fiction which was usually based on real-life figures and events. Backgrounds in her works such as ancient Greece, France, Germany and the West Indies were the result of her extensive travels.

Some of the awards given to Atherton were the National Academy of Literature presidency, a gold medal from the City of San Francisco, and honorary degrees from the University of California and Mills College.

Her books include, *The Californians*, a contrast of cultures, *Before the Gringo Game*, and *Horn of Life*, all about her native state. Other novels appealed to her ideals of women's rights and rejuvenation of older women, in such works as *Julia France and Her Times*, *Black Oxen*, *The Crystal Cup*, and *The Sophisticates*. Much of her writing describes fellow California literary figures of her time, including Ambrose Bierce. Her last books, *Golden Gate Country* and *My San Francisco*, were non-fictional accounts of her birthplace.

•**AUSTIN, MARY (HUNTER)**, (1868-1934) - author, was born in Illinois, but spent most of her life in various parts of California. After moving to the Owens Valley to homestead with her family, she was married to Stafford Austin, manager of an Owens River irrigation project, but the partnership was brief and unhappy.

She began to write sketches of the desert region of the state for the Overland Monthly, which she later collected in *The Land of Little Rain* (1903), which received critical acclaim. Soon she became interested in the Paiute Indians and wrote stories about them, including *The Basket Woman* (1904) and *Isidro*, as well as a poem on sheepherding in the desert valley of California entitled *The Flock*. Soon after these were published, Austin moved to Carmel to form an artists' colony there. She concentrated her writing on nature and primitive Indian life, with an emphasis on mysticism.

After 1912 she moved to New York, and spent the next 12 years living alternately there and in Carmel, and consequently her writings became broader and more political. She wrote essays on feminism and socialism, and novels purporting her ideas on contemporary issues, such as *A Woman of Genius* (1912), and *No. 26 Jayne Street* (1920). *The Ford* (1917), marked Austin's return to Californian issues, this time treating the conflict between real estate investors and social reformers. Throughout her life and works, however, Austin explored her mystical and religious convictions, especially in tales of Jesus Christ, as well as the naturalistic beliefs of the Indians. Her exalting faith in Indian culture brought her back permanently to the west, in Santa Fe (1924), and she often returned to California memories in her works, such as the autobiographical *Earth Horizon* (1932).

•'AVIS, HORACE, (1831-1916) - U. S. representative was born in Worcester, Massachusetts and attended the public schools and Williams College in Williamstown, Massachusetts. He graduated from Harvard University in 1849, studied law in the Dane Law School of Harvard University, but did not engage in professional pursuits by reason of failing eyesight. He moved to California in 1852 and engaged in mercantile pursuits, moving to San Francisco in 1860, he engaged in the flour-milling business. He was elected as a Republican to the forty-fifth and Forty-sixth Congresses (March 4, 1877-March 3, 1881, but was an unsuccessful candidate for reelection in 1880 to the forty-seventh Congress. He resumed his former business pursuits and was a member of the Republican National Committee (1880-1888). President of the chamber of Commerce of San Francisco in 1883 and 1884, he was a presidential elector on the Republican ticket of Blaine and Logan in 1884. In addition, he was president of the board of trustees of Leland Stanford Junior University (1885-1916) and president of the University of California at Berkeley (1887-1890). He died in San Francisco.

B

•**BADHAM, ROBERT EDWARD** (1929-) - U.S. representative from California, was born in Los Angeles, California, and attended Beverly Hills High School and Occidental College (1947-1948), before graduating from Stanford University with a B.A. in 1951. He served in the United States Navy in the early 1950s, and then became a business executive. He was the director of Hoffman Hardware Company from 1952 until 1969. A member of the state Assembly from 1963 to 1976, he was elected as a Republican to the Ninety-fifth Congress on November 2, 1976. Reelected three times, he is a member of the current Ninety-eighth Congress. He is married to Anne Carroll.

•**BALBOA, VASCO NUNEZ DE,** (1475-1517) - explorer, was born in Xeres de los Caballeros, Spain, in 1475. He made his first notable voyage in 1501 when he sailed with Rodergio de Bastidas on an exploratory trip to the west. He moved to Espanola in the West Indies (today known as Haiti and Santo Domingo) and tried farming, but had little success. To avoid paying off the large debts he had incurred, he stowed away on a provision ship bound for San Sebastion. When the explorers arrived there, they found the settlement destroyed. Balboa, by then discovered, suggested to to the ship's captain, Francisco de Enciso, that they head towards Därien on the Gulf of Uraba, an area Balboa had explored on his voyage with Bastidas. Enciso agreed. At Darien, they established the town of Santa Maria de la Antiqua. When Enciso prohibited his crew from trading for gold with the natives, the two explorers began fightly. Balboa and the crew revolted, imprisoning Enciso, and leaving Balboa free to explore the surrounding countryside. On one of these explorations, he was told of the great sea beyond the mountains and of the land where gold was plentiful (Peru). Not long afterwards, Balboa was recalled to Spain because of his actions against Enciso. The explorer, trying to find some way to placate the king, decided to search for that distant sea. Setting off with nearly 200 men, Balboa first sighted the Pacific on September 25, 1513. Three days later, he was at its shore at a place he named Gulf of San Miguel. Claiming the ocean for the king of Spain, he returned in early January to Darien, and sent word to the king of his discovery. Before Balboa's message had reached Spain, however, Dom Pedro Arias de Avila, an envoy of the king, arrived in Darien and had the explorer arrested. After paying a large fine, he was released. The king eventually acknowledged Balboa's discovery, and commissioned him to continue his explorations. Despite his initial distrust of Balboa, Aliva, the governor of Darien, helped the explorer ready for the expedition, and even offered him his daughter's hand in marriage. Balboa set sail before the marriage was made, and Avila again grew distrustful. After capturing the Pearl Islands for Spain, Balboa headed towards Peru's coast, but was forced to abandon the mission because of bad weather. Using a ruse, Avila convinced Balboa to come to Acla. When the explorer arrived, the Darien governor had him arrested on charges of treason. The next day, Balboa and five of his companions were executed.

•BALDWIN, JOHN FINLEY, JR., (1915-1966) - U.S. congressman from California, was born in Oakland, California, and graduated from San Ramon Valley Union High School in Danville, California, and from the University of California at Berkeley (1935), where he majored in accounting and finance. After graduating, he became the assistant manager of South Western Publishing Company of San Francisco from 1936 to 1941, when he enlisted as a private in the United States Army. He served as director of training at the U.S. Army Finance School in 1943 and 1944, and as Chief of Foreign Fiscal Affairs Branch of the War Department's Office of Fiscal Director in 1945. The following year, he was made the Executive Officer, Office of Fiscal Direction, Mediterranean Theatre. He was decorated by the Italian government for work in the devaluation of the lira currency in

1946. After the war, Baldwin entered the University of California Boalt Hall School of Law in Berkeley and was graduated in 1949. After passing the bar, he began practicing in Martinez. In 1954, he was elected as a Republican to the Eighty-fourth Congress. Reelected five times, he served until his death in Washington, D.C.

•BANCROFT, HUBERT HOWE, (1832-1918) - publisher, moved to California in 1852 from Ohio to try to mine and sell books, as he had done in Buffalo, N.Y. In a few years, he has established the best-stocked bookstore in the West in San Francisco. The store grew into a publishing house of sorts, printing law books, legal stationery, texts and maps, music, and colored labels for cans. A firm believer in the free enterprise system, he employed a large staff of salesmen to market his subscription books.

One day in 1859 Bancroft discovered he owned an extensive collection of books on the Pacific Coast and its history. Soon, Bancroft decided to bring together California's history in encyclopedia form, and, realizing that he couldn't do the project alone, hired a staff of assistants for research when the writing project began in 1871. In the end, the project, which took over eight years, was called "Bancroft's Works" and filled 39 volumes, although Bancroft himself wrote only about four of them. However, the bookish entrepreneur represented himself as the sole author of the encyclopedia, and the assistants who received no credit for their work complained. In response to one sour assistant, Bancroft replied, "I doubt that authors are in the habit of giving their employees any credit at all." Bancroft's manner in marketing the encylopedia also caused public criticism of the work. Many purchasers of the work were not told by salesmen exactly how many volumes they were contracting to buy. And a biographical addition to the "Works" was found corrupt when it was discovered that the California figures mentioned in it had paid Bancroft thousands of dollars for the favor. Leland Stanford, founder of the university, refused to pay Bancroft, and consequently was not mentioned in the biographical encyclopedia.

As a result of Bancroft's impropriety, his reputation suffered. When he sold his library to the University of California in 1905, some were skeptical because it cost the university $250,000, although Bancroft claimed he made a gift of $100,000 toward the purchase.

•BAND, MAX, (1900-) - artist, was born in Naumestic, Lithuania, to Abraham and Anna Band and was educated at the Freie Academie in Berlin and the Academie Libre in Paris. He lived in Paris from 1922 to 1940 and came to the United State at the onset of the Second World War, settling in Hollywood, California, with his wife, the former Berthe Finkelstein. A life Fellow of the International Institute of Arts and Letters and an honorary member of the California Art, Band has been the subject of numerous books. He is the author of *Themes from the Bible* and has exhibited widely in the United States and Europe. Considered one of the founders of the originial School of Paris, he has works on display in the permanent collections of the Musee du Jeu de Paume, Musee de Petit Palais, Musee de Ville de Pari, Musee d'Art Moderne, Paris; Musee de Ceret, France; Riverside Museum, New York; Phillips Memorial Gallery, Washington, D.C.; French Art Institute, Philadelphia; Fine Arts Museum, San Diego; and other leading museums worldwide. In 1934, Band was commissioned to paint a portrait of President Franklin Delano Roosevelt.

•BARANOV, ALEXANDER ANDREEVICH, (1747-1819) - fur trader and first governor of Russian America, was the manger of a glass factory in Siberia, before becoming a trader. In 1790, he moved to what is now the Kodiak Islands, Alaska, to become director of the Russian American Company, a fur trading company established by G.I. Shelekov. Shelekov established the company after the sea otter had been driven away from the Aleutian Islands. For many years, the company prospered, but by 1810 the otter had all but disappeared from Alaska's coastline. In 1811,

Baranov headed to the California coast to hunt the otter there. For three years, he remained in California, before returning north. In 1818, nine years after he asked to be replaced, he stepped down from his position and headed home to Russia. He died on the voyage there.

•BARBOUR, HENRY ELLSWORTH, (1877-1945) - U.S. congressman from California, was born in Ogdensburg, New York, and attended the local public schools before entering Union College at Schenectady. He also studied law at George Washington University. After being admitted to the New York bar in 1901, he moved west to Fresno, California, where he began practicing law. In 1918, he was elected as a Republican to the Sixty-sixth Congress. Reelected six times, he was finally defeated in a reelection bid in 1932. When his last term expired the following year, he returned to his law practice. He died in Fresno.

•BARD, THOMAS ROBERT, (1841-1915) - U.S. congressman from California and one of the founders of Ventura County, was born in Chambersburg, Pennsylvania, and attended the local common schools before before graduating from Chambersburg Academy in 1858. He studied law briefly, but before completing his studies, he secured a position with the Pennsylvania Railroad Company. Later, he became assistant to the superintendent of the Cumberland Valley Railroad and had charge of the movement of trains carrying military supplies. He also worked in a grain business in Hagerstown, Maryland. During the early part of the Civil War, he served as a volunteer Union scout while the Confederate troops were invading Maryland and Pennsylvania. In 1864, he moved to Ventura County, California. Four years later, he became a member of the San Barbara County Board of Supervisors, a position he retained for five years. He helped lay out the town of Hueneme and he was one of the commissioners appointed to organize Ventura County in 1871. From 1886 to 1887, he was the director of the state board of agriculture. In 1892, he was the only presidential elector chosen on the Republican ticket of Harrison and Reed, the other electors being democrat. He was elected as a Republican to the United States Senate to fill a vacancy in the term beginning in 1899. After being defeated in a reelection bid in 1904, he stepped down from office in 1905. He died at his home in Hueneme.

•BARHAM, JOHN ALL, (1843-1926) - U.S. congressman from California, was born in Cass County, Missouri, and moved with his parents to Woodland, California, in 1849. He attended the common schools and Hesperian College before he began teaching public school in 1864. He continued to teach until 1876. At the same time, he began studying law, and in 1865, he was admitted to the state bar. Over the next several years, he practiced in Watsonville, San Francisco and Santa Rosa. He was elected as a Republican to the Fifty-fourth Congress in 1894. Reelected twice, he did not seek renomination in 1900. After leaving office, he continued to practice law in Santa Rosa until his death there twenty-six years later.

•BARLOW, CHARLES AVERILL, (1858-1927) - U.S. congressman from California, was born in Cleveland, Ohio, and attended the common schools. He engaged in agricultural and commerical pursuits for a time before moving in 1875 to Ventura, California, where he engaged in wheat farming. After moving to San Luis Obispo County in 1889, he became a member of the state assembly and served from 1892 to 1893. Chairman of the People's Party State convention in 1896, Barlow was elected as a Populist and Democrat to the Fifty-fifth Congress and served from 1897 to 1899. He was not a candidate for renomination. In 1901, he moved to Kern County where he was engaged in mining, fruit growing, and oil production. He was a delegate to the Democratic National Conventions in 1912 and 1920. He died in Bakersfield.

•BARTLETT, WASHINGTON, (1824-1887) - sixteenth governor of California (1887), was born in Savannah, Georgia, the eldest son of Cosam E. and Sarah F. Bartlett. His ancestors on his father's side came from England early in the seventeenth century, and settled in the village of Newbury, Mass. His great-grandfather, Stephen Bartlett, was eldest brother of Josiah Bartlett, governor of New Hampshire, and a signer of the Declaration of Independence.

Washington Bartlet grew up in Georgia and Tallahassee, Fla., where he obtained a fair education, mostly in private schools. In November, 1849, he arrived in San Francisco, and immediately engaged in the printing business and published the first book printed in California--*California as It Is and as It May Be: A Guide to the Gold Region* (1849). In January 1850, he started the "Daily Journal of Commerce," and vigorously advocated the "Compromise Measures" of 1850, including the admission of California as a state. He was a leader in the uprising of 1856, being a member of the "Vigilance Committee" and captain of an artillery company composed of "Vigilantes."

He was elected county clerk of San Francisco county in 1859 and reelected three times; was chosen state senator in 1873 and served four years. In 1882 he was elected mayor of San Francisco, and again in 1884, serving two full terms. In 1886 he was chosen governor of California although most of the candidates on the Democratic ticket, including the candidate for lieutenant-governor, were defeated. He was inaugurated on Jan. 8, 1887, and held office until his death. Governor Bartlett was a conspicuous figure in California life--in its politics and business enterprises, and exercised great influence in shaping the history of the state. Although successful in business he never allowed his fortune to accumulate beyond $100,000, nor his private expenses to exceed $200 per month--the excess was systematically devoted to charity and assisting relatives and friends. He was never married, and died Sept. 12, 1887.

•BEALE, EDWARD FITZGERALD, (1822-18) - surveyor general of California and the U.S. minister to Austria, was born in Washington, D.C., and studied at Georgetown College. In 1842, he graduated from the U.S. Naval Academy. During the war with Mexico, Beale, then a lieutenant, fought beside General Stephen Kearny and Kit Carson in the campaign to wrest control of Los Angeles from the Californian army. At one point during the campaign, when Kearny was leading his troops northward from San Diego, the Americans were met by the troops of Gen. Andres Pico and nearly surrounded. The battle that ensued was one of the worst in California's history. Although his troops were able to hold off the Californians, Kearny did not have enough men to advance further. Three of Kearny's men - Beale, Carson and an unnamed Indian - volunteered to return to San Diego to seek aide from Gen. Robert Stockton. Through the skill of Carson, the three eluded the besiegers and made their way to the southern port town. Stockton responded to Kearny's call for aid with 180 men. A few weeks later, the war ended. Beale was awarded a sword by his fellow officers for his gallantry. Soon afterwards, Beale was named superintendent of Indian Affairs for California and New Mexico. In 1861, he was appointed surveyor general of California, but resigned the post to return to military duty at the outbreak of the Civil War. He was appointed U.S. minister to Austria in 1875, and served in that capacity for two years before returning to California to devote his final years to ranching. Beale Air Force Base in Yuba County is named for him.

•BELL, ALPHONZO, (1914-) - U.S. congressman from California, was born in Los Angeles, California, and attended Hawthorned Grammar and Webb schools. He graduated from Occidental College in 1938, and during World War Two, he served in the U.S. Army Air Corps (1942-1945). After the war ended, he was engaged in ranching, real estate and the petroleum industry. He was president of Bell Petroleum Company from 1947 to 1960. Since 1960, he has been chairman of the board of the petroleum company. From 1956 to 1958, he was chairman of the Republican State Central Committee of California and a member of the Republican National Committee. In 1958, he became chairman of the Republican Central Committee of Los Angeles. He remained in that position until 1960, when he was elected as a Republican to the Eighty-seventh Congress. He served in the U.S. House of Representative until 1977.

•BELL, CHARLES WEBSTER, (1857-1927) - U.S. congressman from California, was born in Albany, New York, and attended the public schools. He moved to California in 1877 and settled in Pasadena, where he engaged in fruit growing and the real estate business. Bell was county clerk of Los Angeles County from 1899 to 1903 and a member of the state senate from 1907 to 1912. Elected as a Progressive Republican to the Sixty-third Congress in 1912, he was defeated in a reelection bid two years later. After leaving office in 1915, he resumed his earlier business pursuits in Pasadena, where he later served as secretary of the Pasadena Mercantile Finance Corporation. He died in Pasadena.

•BELL, THEODORE ARLINGTON, (1872-1922) - U.S. congressman from California, was born in Vallejo, California, and was reared predominantly in St. Helena, where he attended the public schools. After studying law, he was admitted to the bar in 1893 and began practicing in Napa. He served as district attorney of Napa County from 1895 until 1903, when he was elected as a Democrat to the Fifty-eighth Congress. Defeated in a reelection bid two years later, he moved to San Francisco and resumed practicing law. Bell was an unsuccessful candidate for governor in 1906 and 1910. He was a delegate to the Democratic National Convention in Denver in 1908 and served temporarily as chairman. He was also a delegate to the convention in Baltimore four years later. Not long after joining the Republican Party in 1921, he was accidentally killed near San Rafael, California.

•BEILENSON, ANTHONY CHARLES (1932-) - U.S. representative from California, was born in New Rochelle, New York, and attended William Wilson Grammar School in Mount Vernon, New York. He graduated from Phillips Academy in Andover, Massachussetts (1950), Harvard College (A.B. 1954), and Harvard Law School (LL.B 1957). A member of the California Assembly (1963-1966) and the state Senate (1967-1977), he was elected to the Ninety-Fifth Congress in 1976 and has been reelected to each succeeding Congress, including the current Ninety-eighth. He married Dolores Martin in 1959.

•BENEDICT, HENRY STANLEY, (1878-1930) - U.S. congressman from California, was born in Boonville, Missouri, and moved with his parents in 1888 to Los Angeles, where he attended grammar and high school. After studying at the University of South California College of Law, he was admitted to the bar in 1910 and began practing law in Los Angeles. He was a member of the state house of representative from 1910 until 1914, when he was elected to the state senate. Two years later, he was elected as a Republican to the Sixty-fourth Congress to fill the vacancy caused by the resignation of William D. Stephens. Though he was nominated for the Sixty-fifth Congress by the Progressive Party, he withdrew his name in behalf of the Republican nominee. After leaving office in 1917, he continued to practice law, while also engaging in banking. He was a member of the state department of finance of California from 1919 until 1921, when he was named to the California State Railroad Commission. In 1923, he left the commission and once again returned to practicing law in Los Angeles. He died while on a visit in London, England.

•BERRY, CAMPBELL POISON, (1834-1901) - U.S. congressman from California, was born in Jackson County, Alabama, and moved with his parents in 1841 to Berryville, Arkansas, where he attended grammar school. He moved to California in 1857 and settled near Yuba City. A year after he graduated from the Pacific Methodist College in Vacaville, California, in 1865, he became a supervisor of Sutter County. He left the supervisor position in 1869 and became engaged in agricultural pursuits. He was also in the mercantile business in 1872. A member of the state assembly for many years, he was elected as a Democrat to the Forty-sixth and Forty-seventh Congresses, and served from 1879 to 1883. He did not seek a third term. From 1894 to 1898, he was subtreasurer of the United States at San Francisco. He died in Wheatland.

•BIDWELL, JOHN, (1819-1900) - U.S. congressman from California, was born in Chautauqua County, New York, and moved with his parent to Erie, Pennsylvania, in 1829, and to Ashtabula County, Ohio, in 1831. He attended the country schools and Kingsville Academy in Ashtabula and then began teaching. After spending two years working in Missouri, he crossed the Rockies and Sierras and settled in 1841 in the Sacramento Valley, where he secured employment on the ranch of John A. Sutter. Later, he engaged in mining. He served with the American army during the war with Mexico and attained the rank of major. When the war ended, he was a member of the state constitutional convention and a state senator (1849). In both 1850 and 1860, he was a supervisor in California of the United States census. Bidwell was a delegate to the Republican National Convention at Baltimore in 1860. During the Civil War, he was appointed brigadier general of the California Militia. He was a delegate to the Republican National Convention at Baltimore in 1864 when Lincoln and Johnson were nominated. That same year he was elected as a Unionist to the Thirty-nineth Congress, but was not a candidate for renomination two years later. He was an unsuccessful candidate for governor in 1875 on the Anti-Monopoly ticket, and in 1890 as Prohibition State candidate. In 1892, he was the Prohibition State candidate for president. He died in Chico.

•BIERCE, AMBROSE, (1842-c1913) - author, was born on a farm in Meiggs County, Ohio, to Marcus Aurelius Bierce and Laura Sherwood Bierce. The youngest of eight children, Bierce began reading at an early age and received his first formal education at a nearby district school. In his teens, he developed a close relationship with his uncle, General Lucius Verus Bierce, an adament anti-slavery leader and a close friend of John Brown of Harper's Ferry fame. At 15 Bierce attended Kentucky Military Institute for one term where he developed a talent for cartooning. After leaving the institute, he became a printer's apprentice at a small Indiana newspaper.

At 18, he enlisted in the Indiana volunteers to fight in the Civil War. Although wounded in the head early in his military career, he was discharged as a major after four years of service.

Moving to San Francisco, he contributed a few stories to local magazines and was hired to edit a financial newspaper in the city, *The News Letter*, where in 1868, he began his career as a satirist writing a humor column called "The Town Crier." He married Molly Day in 1870 and moved to London in 1872. During his three years in England, his reputation grew as he wrote three books and contributed regularly to a humor magazine, *London Fun.* Returning to San Francisco in 1875, he began editing *The Argonaut,* but his ideas were too controversial for the conservative publication. Instead, he edited a political humor magazine (1881-1886). His brilliance at a peak, he contributed verse, short story, features, editorials and cartoons to the magazine. Sent to Washington, D.C. in 1896 by the San Francisco *Examiner* to help defeat a controversial railroad bill, he soon established permanent residence there. Writing as a national columnist in William R. Hearst newspapers, he was also the literary critic of *Cosmopolitan* magazine. Resigning from the Hearst publication in 1908, he spent the remainder of his life working on his short stories. In 1912 and 1913, he visited revolution-torn Mexico. Sometime in 1913, he disappeared there. Among his works were *Tales of Soldiers and Civilians* (1891), his first volume of short stories; *The Devil's Dictionary* (1884); and a 10 volume complete works *Collected Works of Ambrose Bierce* (1912).

•BIERSTADT, ALBERT, (1830-1920) - artist, was born in Dusseldorf, Germany, to Henry and Christian M. Bierstadt. At two, he immigrated with his family to New Bedford, Massachusetts. He moved back to Dusseldorf in 1853 to study art. During his free summer months, he would travel to the mountains of Switzerland and Germany to draw sketches of the magnificent landscape. He returned to America after four years abroad, and soon joined an expedition heading west to the Rockies. It was the paintings from this trip that first brought Beirstadt prominence in the art world as one of the pioneers of Western Art. Some of his most famous paintings, however, were drawn years later from settings in California. He also returned to Europe four times and made a voyage to the West Indies to gather background material for a historical painting on Columbus. Over the years, he received numerous honors and awards, including France's Legion of Honor decoration (1867), and Russia's Order of Saint Stanislaus (1869). England elected him a

National Academician, and he was a member of the U.S. National Academy of Design. Among his more prominent work are, "Discovery of the Hudson River", "Settlement of California", "Domes of Yosemite", "Storm on the Matterhon", and "The Last of the Buffalo." He married Rosalie Osborne in 1866. Rosalie died in 1893, and during the following year, he married Mrs. Stewart. He died in New York City.

•BIGLER, JOHN, (1804-1871) - third governor of California (1852-1856), was born in Cumberland county, Pennsylvania, of German paarentage. He received a public school education, learned the printer's trade, and was the editor of the *Center Democrat*, at Bellefonte, Pennsylvania, for several years. During this time he studied law, was admitted to the bar, and practiced his profession with considerable success. In 1846 he settled in Illinois, but was one of the first of the "Argonauts of 1849" to reach California.

He was an approachable, good-natured, neighborly man, who was willing to labor with his hands when it seemed necessary. He had unloaded steamboats, cut wood, taken a contract for making bedding and sold goods under the hammer in an auction store. He had the essential elements of personal popularity for such a community as that of early California.

Bigler was inaugurated governor of California January 8, 1852, and in this capacity ministered largely to the wants of immigrants, many of whom reached the state in a forlorn and even suffering condition. During his administration an attempt was made in the state legislature to introduce the coolie system of labor, but it was defeated by indefinite postponement. Governor Bigler urged retrenchment, and for the revision of the revenue laws. The statutes regarding the collection of taxes were imperfect, and delinquencies by state officials were not uncommon. But the governor was unable to stem the tide of misrule. He was himself charged with corruption. He was chosen to a second term in 1853.

In April, 1854, a United States mint went into operation at San Francisco. About this time measures were taken by the Congress to begin the construction of the national navy-yard, at Mare

Island, California, and in 1856, the last year of Governor Bigler's incumbency, appropriations for this project were approved. Governor Bigler was nominated by the Democrats for a third term, but was defeated.

•BOAZ, MARTHA, (1914-) - educator, was born in Stuart, Virginia, to Kate Gilley and James Robert Boaz. After graduating from Stuart High School, she studied English at Madison College (B.S., 1935). In 1950, she received an M.A. in library sciences from the University of Michigan and five years later she received her Ph.D. in that field from University of Michigan. Her first position was as a teacher in a school in Bridgewater. Virginia, from 1935 to 1937, when she moved to Jeffersontown, Kentucky, to teach both English and Latin in a high school. Three years later she returned to Virginia to become assistant librarian at Madison College in Harrisonburg. In 1950 to 1951, she was associate professor of library service at the University of Tennessee, and while studying at the University of Michigan, she was an instructor of library science (1951-1952). The next year, she was a librarian in the public service department of the Pasadena Public Library in California, but she went, in 1953, to the University of Southern California to be an associate professor (1953-1955). She was then promoted to dean and full professorship at USC, which she held until 1979. At that time, Boaz joined the Center for the Study of American Experience at the University as a research associate. Boaz had written several books on library management and usage and she was a consultant to Encyclopedia Brittanica from 1962 to 1964 and 1972 to 1974. She has been a member of the editorial board of the magazine, *Highlights for Children* since 1957. She has also worked with the United States government in helping develop libraries in Pakistan (1962) and Vietnam (1966) and wrote about it for the *Journal of Education for Librarianship* in 1967 in the article "The American Library Specialist in an Underdeveloped Country." She has also evaluated the library systems in several southern California cities as well as Port Angeles, Washington. She was president of the Association of American Library Schools from 1962 to 1963, as well as the American Documentation Institute of Southern California (1962) and the California Library Association (1962).

In 1970 Boaz planned and moderated a part of the Emmy-award winning "Odyssey" television series produced by USC's College of Continuing Education. Her segment was entitled "The Living Library," and was shown on a local CBS channel. Her books include: *Issues in Higher Education and the Professions* (1981), *Strategies for Meeting the Information Needs of Society in the Year 2000* (1981), Current Concepts in Library Management, (ed.), (1979), *Fervent and Full of Gifts, the Life of Althea Warren* (1961), *A Guide to General Book Publishers in the United States* (1960), *A Living Library* (1958), and *Modern Trends in Documentation* 1959).

•BOGGS, LILBURN W. (1798-1861) - fifth governor of Missouri (1837-41) and early California leader, was born in Kentucky. Moving to Missouri, he worked for several years as a cashier in the Bank of St. Louis before entering politics. He was elected lieutenant-governor in 1832, and became governor of the state five years later when the acting governor resigned. Later that year, he was elected for a full term to that office. Boggs was instrumental during his tenure in the removal of the Mormons from Missouri. The project, however, made him the target of an unsuccessful assassination attempt in which he received three gun shot wounds to the head and chest. He moved to California in 1846, five years after stepping down as governor, and was appointed alcalde over the Sonoma district. In that post, he was instrumental in bringing Sonoma into the United States. He died in Sacramento.

•BOOTH, NEWTON, (1825-1878) - eleventh governor of California (1872-1874) and United States Senator, was born at Salem, Indiana, graduated from Asbury University in 1846, studied law at Terre Haute, Indiana, and was admitted to the bar in that city in 1850. The same year he moved to California, engaging in the wholesale grocery business in Sacramento. Returning to Terre Haute in 1857, he practiced law there until 1860, when he returned to California.

In 1863 he was a member of the state Senate and in 1871 he was chosen governor as an anti-monopolist on an independent ticket, but under Republican auspices. In company with Eugene Casserly, he headed the campaign against the railroad companies. His second biennial report, presented to the legislature in 1873, showed that he was thoroughly acquainted with the finances, resources, and needs of the commonwealth. This document contained statistics showing a large decrease in the indebtedness of the state and called particular attention to the Chinese problem, urging that adequate protection be given the Chinese then in California, but asserting that unless measures be taken to restrict further immigration, society would be modified, and the relations between capital and labor changed.

In March, 1874, Booth was elected to the United States Senate by the anti-monopolists, and accordingly resigned the governorship. He served a full term in the Senate (1875-1881), and then returned to California to resume his business life. He died on July 14, 1892 in Sacramento.

•BOWERS, WILLIAM, (1834-1917) - U.S. congressman from California, was born in Whitestown, New York, where he attended the public schools before moving to Wisconsin in 1854. In 1862, he enlisted as a private in Company I, First Wisconsin Calvary, and was discharged three years later as a second sergeant. He moved to San Diego in 1869 and began ranching. He was a member of the state assembly in 1873 and 1874 and served as collector of customs at the port of San Diego from 1874 until 1879. He owned and operated a hotel in San Diego from 1884 through 1891, and served as a member of the state senate from 1887 to 1889. Two years later he was elected as a Republican to the Fifty-second Congress. Reelected twice, he was defeated in 1896 in a bid for a fourth term in office. In 1902, he was again appointed collector of customs for the San Diego port. He remained in that positon until 1906, when he retired. He died in San Diego.

•BRAMBLETT, ERNEST KING, (1901-1966) - U.S. congressman from California, was born in Fresno, California, and attended the public schools. He gradutated from Stanford University in 1925 and later took graduate work there and at Fresno State, San Jose State and the University ofSouthern California. He worked in the insurance and automobile industries from 1925 until 1928, when he began working in education. He continued to do educational work until 1946. Over the years he was mayor of Pacific Groves (1939-1947), coordinator of Monterey County Schools (1943-1946), and a member of the Republican Central Committee (1944-1946). In 1946, he was elected as a Republican to the Eightieth Congress. Reelected three time, he was not a candidate for renomination in 1954. When his final term expired in 1955, he became a consultant in Southern California, which he continued to do until his death in Woodland Hills eleven years later.

•BRANNAN, SAMUEL, (1819-1889) - pioneer and early Mormon leader, was born in Saco, Maine. He moved to Lake County, Ohio, when he was fourteen and began studying the printer's trade. After converting to Mormonism in 1842, he moved to New York City and began publishing the New York Messenger and the New York Prophet, two Mormon journals. Four years later, he lead a group of 238 Mormons around the tip of South America to San Francisco. For twenty years, Brannan was a powerful figure in San Francisco, as a member of the city council and as a large landholder. In 1847, he established the city's first newspaper, the California Star, and later was a principal organizer of the city's vigilantes. He moved to Sutter's Fort in 1847 and opened a store, but two years later, he returned to San Francisco. Bra'nnon tried to induce Brigham Young to abandon Utah and settle in California, but the Mormon leader would not. Over the years, Brannon and Young continually bickered over the disposition of tithes collected by Brannan from the Mormons in California. On several occasions, Young sent his Destroying Angels to seize them by force, but they were never successful. Although he amassed a fortune, Brannan became a drunkard and died in poverty in Escondido, California.

•BRODERICK, DAVID C., (1820-1859) - United States Senator from California, was born in Washington D.C., the son of an Irish immigrant stonemason. When, as a boy, Broderick watched his father at work on ornamentation for the Senate chambers, he resolved to return there to speak. His family moved to New York City, where he became a saloon keeper and a ward boss for Tammany Hall, but he was unsuccessful in his attempt for a Congress seat. He was convinced by friends to move to San Francisco and set up a Democratic political machine such as that at Tammany. He also made a small fortune by minting counterfeit coins with stated face values far above their gold content.

In 1850, Broderick was elected to the state senate, and later became the senate's presiding officer. By 1857, he had convinced the legislature to elect him to an unprecedented six year term as a U. S. senator, a triumph over his arch political rival, senior Senator William M. Gwin. However, two years later Gwin's pro-slavery group took over the majority of open positions in a state election, which outraged Broderick. When California Chief Justice David S. Terry aligned himself in a campaign speech with Gwin's faction, Broderick called him a "damned miserable wretch," who was as corrupt as the other members of the supreme court. When Terry failed to win renomination, he challenged Broderick to a duel, in which Broderick was fatally wounded.

At Broderick's eulogy, admirers claimed he was killed because he was "opposed to a corrupt administration and the extension of slavery."

•BROWN, AARON VAIL, (1795-1859) - governor of Tennessee (1846-48) and postmaster general, was born in Brunswick County, Virginia, to Rev. Aaron Brown, a Methodist preacher, and Elizabeth Melton. The younger Brown graduated from the University of North Carolina, Chapel Hill, at the age of nineteen as valedictorian. In 1815, Brown began studying law in Nashville. He returned to Giles in 1817, the year after he was admitted into the bar, and began practicing with James K. Polk, the future U.S. President. In 1821, Brown was elected to the state senate, yet he continued to practice law until 1839, when he was elected to Congress. Reelected twice as a representative, Brown was elected governor of Tennessee in 1845, and held that office for two years. With the election of James Buchanan as president, Brown was appointed postmaster-general in 1857. During his tenure as postmaster he was instrumental in improving the mail service to California. He established a route by way of the Great Salt Lake, another by way of the isthmus of Tehuantepec, and a third overland from Memphis to St. Louis and San Francisco. He died in Washington, D.C.

•BROWN, EDMUND GERALD, (1905-) - thirty-second Governor of California 1958-1967), born in San Francisco on April 21, 1905. His parents were Edmund J. and Ida (Shuckman) Brown.   He worked as a clerk in his father's store after from Lowell High School while attending San Francisco College of Law, He married Bernice Layne on October 30, 1930 and has four children. His only son, Edmund G. Jr., became thirty-fourth Governor of California   At first a Republican he changed to the Democratic Party in 1934 and won election as Attorney General in 1950 on that ticket. Brown defeated William Knowland, the Republican, in 1958 to become only the second Democratic Governor in the twentieth century. For his second term Brown defeated Republican Richard M. Nixon (1962). Brown was nicknamed "Patrick Henry" or "Pat" because of a speech he made for World War I Bonds. During his administration he undertook administrative reforms and reapportionment and established new goals for higher education as well as other significant social services under a program he termed "responsible liberalism." Brown was defeated for a third term by Ronald Reagan by one million votes   Now a resident of Beverly Hills, he has authored several introspective political works including: *Regan and Reality: The Two Californians* (New York 1970).

•BROWN, EDMUND GERALD, JR., (1938-) - thirty-fourth governor of California, was born in San Franicsco. A fourth generation Californian, and son of former Governor Edmund,

Sr., he is generally referred to as Jerry Brown. Considering becoming a Jesuit priest, Brown studied at the Sacred Heart Novitiate in Los Gatos and at the University of Santa Clara. Later, he received a degree in the classics at the University of California, Berkeley, and took a law degree from Yale. One of the few Democrats to win in the 1970 state election, Brown became Secretary of State.   Brown ran twice for the Democratic nomination for the presidency while he was governor. In 1976, he campaigned up to the Democratic National Convention, but in early 1980 he dropped out of the race when he won only one delegate after a series of primary elections. Proclaiming his ideas for a "new age" in politics, Brown said he quit because the public "was not ready for me yet."

The governor was famous for his unconventional lifestyle, refusing to live in the mansions in Sacramento and Carmichael in favor of a small apartment, and limiting his state speeches to under ten minutes. He was often criticized for using buzz words in statements to the media, and newspapers featured his interests in all aspects of alternative culture, including health foods and Zen Buddhism. Probably because of the image projected of him in the media, Brown was not successful in his 1982 attempt for a U.S. Senator seat. Republican critics blamed Brown for the state's huge budget deficits when he left office, but political observers later pointed to the passage of tax cuts and the general economic recession for most of the financial problems. Brown has claimed that he is not finished with politics since he left the governorship in January 1983.

•BROWN, GEORGE E., JR. (1920-) - U.S. representative from California, was born in Holtville, California, and graduated from the University of California at Los Angeles with a B.A. in industrial physics. Employed by the city of Los Angeles for twelve years in personnel, engineering, and management positions, he later worked as a management consultant. During the second World War, he was a second lieutenant in the United States infantry. He was the mayor and a city council for Monterey Park from 1954 to 1958, and a state assemblyman from 1959 to 1962. Elected as a Democrat to the Ninety-third Congress on November 7, 1972, he has been reelected to each succeeding Congress through the current Ninety-eighth Congress. He is married to Rowena Somerindyke.

•BUCK, FRANK HENRY, (1887-1942) - U.S. congressman from California, was born on a ranch near Vacaville, California, and graduated from the University of California at Berkeley in 1908 and from the law department of Harvard University in Cambridge, Massachusetts, in 1911. Admitted to the bar later that year, he began practicing law in San Francisco. Over the years, he was a fruit grower and farmer in Vacaville, and he was also involved in the lumber and oil refining industries. Buck was a delegate to the Democratic National Conventions in 1928, 1936, and 1940. In 1932, he was elected as a Democrat to the Seventy-third Congress. Reelected four times, he served from March, 1933, until his death in Washington a little over nine years later.

•BUDD, JAMES HERBERT, (1851-1908) - nineteenth governor of California (1895-1899), was born in Janesville, Wisconsin, to Joseph H. and Lucinda M. (Ashe) Budd, both natives of New York State. As a child he moved with his parents to Stockton, California. He graduated at the University of California in 1873, then returned to Stockton and studied law in the office of his father, who was a prominent attorney in San Joaquin County, and who subsequently was a state superior judge in that County. In 1882 he was elected to Congress. The climate of Washington affected his health, and he declined a renomination.

Returning to Stockton he resumed his law practice. He served as police and fire commissioner, trustee of the public library, and member of the board of freeholders for drafting the city charter. In 1894 he was nominated for governor and was elected by an overwhelming Democratic majority. During his term the state constitution was amended to require voters to be able to write their own names and to read the Constitution in English; a new banking act was passed, and laws were made in aid of the dairy industry and to prohibit adulteration of drugs, foods and drinks.   Governor Budd was married in 1873, to Inez A. Merrill. At the expiration of his term he retired to his home in Stockton where he died on July 30, 1908.

•BURGENER, CLAIR W. (1921-) - U.S. representative from California, was born in Vernal, Utah, and graduated from Granite High School (1939) and California State University, San Diego, (A.B. 1950). He served in the United States Air Force during the second World War and was awarded an Air Medal in 1945. During the Korean conflict, he was recalled for duty. After the conflict ended, he was a city councilman in San Diego (1953-1957), the city's vice mayor (1955-1956), a state assemblyman (1962-1966), and a state senator (1966-1972). Active in a number of humanitarian groups, he served also as vice chairman of the President's Committee on Mental Retardation and as a member of the National Advisory Committee on Handicapped Children. He was elected as a Republican to the Ninety-third Congress on November 7, 1972, and was reelected to each succeeding Congress, before leaving office at the end of the Ninety-seventh Congress in 1983. He married Marvia Hobusch in 1941.

•BURKE, JOHN HARLEY, (1894-1951) - U.S. congressman from California, was born in Excelsior, Wisconsin, and moved with his parents in 1897 to Milaca, Minnesota, and in 1900 to San Pedro, California. The family moved again in 1909 to Long Beach, where the young Burke attended the public schools and graduated from Long Beach Polytechnic High School in 1913. After attending the University of Santa Clara and the law department of the University of Southern California, he was admitted to the bar in 1917 and began practicing law in Long Beach. During the First World War, he served as a private first class in the Twelfth Training Battery, Field Artillery, at Camp Taylor, Kentucky. After the war ended, he became engaged in the oil business as an independent producer. In 1932, he was elected as a Democrat to to the Seventy-third Congress. He did not seek reelection. When his term expired in 1935, he entered the real estate business in Long Beach, and continued in that field until his death there more than sixteen years later.

•BURKE, YVONNE BRATHWAITE, (1932) - U. S. representative from California, was born in Los Angeles, the daughter of Lola Moore, a real estate agent, and James T. Watson, a janitor, and attended public schools in East Los Angeles before transferring to a school for bright high school students at the University of Southern California. She studied at the University of California, Berkeley and Los Angeles and received a B.A. degree from U.C.L.A. in 1953 in political science and a J.D. from University of Southern California in 1956. Yvonne once admitted to the California bar, Burke, then Watson, began practicing in Los Angeles, specializing in civil, probate, and real estate law.

She married mathematician Louis Brathwaite, in 1957 but the union lasted only seven years. In the meantime, she built up her reputation as a capable lawyer.

In 1965, she witnessed the Watts riots in Los Angeles and became a prominent defender of the rioters. She was also on the McCone Commission to investigate the causes of the uprising, concentrating on the need for better housing in the Los Angeles ghetto. She had become active in the Democratic party when Lyndon Johnson campaigned in 1964, and in 1966 she won a seat in the California legislature over seven male opponents. She was reelected two more times and in 1971 was named chairman of the Urban Development and Housing Commission. In 1972 she was chosen as vice chair of Democratic National Convention in Miami. That same year, in November, she won a seat in the United States House of Representatives for a new district in southwest Los Angeles. One year after taking office, Burke gave birth to a baby girl, Autumn, and became the first congresswoman to take a maternity leave. Reelected to two more sessions of Congress, she was chair of the congressional Black Caucus.

In 1978, she left Washington to campaign for California attorney general. She lost, but continued her involvement in southern California politics. In the meantime, she served on the John F. Kennedy School of Government at Harvard and was a trustee for the University of California. She married William Burke in 1972.

•BURKHALTER, EVERETT GLENN, (1897-1975) - U.S. congressman from California, was born in Heber Springs, Arkansas, and was educated in public schools of Arkansas, Indiana, Colorado, and California. He was an electrical and illuminating engineer in the motion picture industry. In 1918, he enlisted in the United States Navy. Honorably discharged one year later, he remained an active reserve until 1921. He was first elected to public office as a California state assemblyman, serving from 1942 until 1952, when he was elected to the Los Angeles City Council. He served on the city council until 1962, when he was elected as Democrat to the Eighty-eighth Congress. He resigned two years later in disgust with Congress's seniority system. After leaving office, he retired to his home in North Hollywood.

•BURNETT, CORDAS CHRIS, (1917-1975) - educator, was born in Mounds, Illinois, to Christopher C. and Lucy V. Burnett and graduated from De Paul University, Chicago, with a B.A. Awarded an honorary degree from South Eastern Bible College of Birmingham, Alabama, in 1958, he also studied at Washington University in St. Louis, Missouri. Ordained in the Assemblies of God in 1937, he was a minister in several midwestern cities until 1959, when he was appointed president of Bethany Bible College in Santa Cruz, California. He left the school thirteen years later to become executive vice president of the Assemblies of God Graduate School, Theology and Missions, in Springfield, Missouri, where he remained until his death. A member of the Board of Administration of the National Association of Evangelicals, Rev. Burnett was also on the Board of Education of the Assemblies of God in Springfield and was president of the Scotts Valley County Water District. From 1956 to 1975, he was secretary of the evangelical association.

•BURNETT, PETER HARDEMAN, (1807-1895) - first governor of California (1849-1851), was born in Nashville, Tennessee. He practiced law in Missouri before traveling to Oregon in 1843. There he helped organize a territorial government, and although he originally left for California to mine for gold, he soon quit to serve in politics. He gained connections to prominent men in the state, such as Sutter's son, and was appointed a superior court judge by the military governor, General Riley. In a later state supreme court position, Burnett ruled that a slave brought to the free territory of California should be returned to his master, although the southern gentleman had forfeited his legal right to do so when he brought him there. This decision was widely ridiculed, and the slave was eventually freed by the federal government. As governor, Burnett attempted to pass legislation barring free Blacks from the state. He also told legislators that the dwindling number of Indians was "beyond the power of reason of man," and that a "war of extermination will continue to be waged between the races until the Indian race becomes extinct."

In 1851, he resumed his law practice in San Francisco and six years later he was appointed a justice of the state supreme court, but resigned within a year. He wrote two autobiographical works, *The Path Which Led a Protestant Lawyer to the Catholic Church* (1860), and *Recollections and Opinions of an Old Pioneer* (1880).

•BURNHAM, GEORGE, (1868-1939) - U.S. congressman from California, was born in London, England, and immigrated in 1881 to the United States with his parents, who settled in Spring Valley, Minnesota. He was employed as a clerk from 1884 to 1886, before moving to Jackson, Minnesota, in 1887. He worked in Jackson in the retail shoe business until 1901, when he moved again, this time to Spokane, Washington, where he began working in real estate and ranching. In 1903, he moved to San Diego, California. He continued in real estate until 1917 when he took up banking. One of the organizers of the Panama-California Exposition in 1909, he was also a member of the Honorary Commerical Commission to China in 1910, the San Diego Library Commission from 1926 to 1932, and the San Diego Scientific Library from 1926 to 1932. In the latter year, he was elected as a Republican to the Seventy-third Congress. Reelected two years later, he was not a candidate in 1936. When his last term expired, he retired to his home in San Diego. He died in San Diego.

•BURCH, JOHN CHILTON, (1826-1885) - U.S. congressman from California, was born in Boone County, Missouri, and attended Bonne Femme Academy and Kemper College before studying law in Jefferson City. After he was admitted to the bar, he began practicing in his home state. Over the next few years, he served as clerk of Cole County, and then as assistant adjtant general of Missouri. In 1850, he moved to California and began working in the mines. In 1851, he was elected clerk of the newly organized Trinity County. Two years later, he was appointed district attorney. Burch was a member of the state assembly in 1956 and the state senate from 1957 until 1959, when he began serving his only term in the United States House of Representatives. When he stepped down from office two years later, he resumed practicing law in San Francisco. Later, he was appointed as a code commissioner. He declined to be a candidate for judge of the supreme court of California. He died in San Francisco.

•BURTON, C. GRANT, (1916-) - educator, was born in Ogden, Utah, to C.W. and May May Burton and attended Weber State College (A.A. 1936), University of Utah (B.A. 1938, M.A. 1940), and the University of Southern California (Ph.D 1954). During the Second World War, Burton was decorated for his valor, receiving the Bronze Star Medal, Bronze Arrowhead, and Croix De Guerre with Vermillion Star. He taught at several schools before he was hired as executive dean of Institutional Studies at San Jose State University in 1954. Twenty years later he was made executive dean emeritus. He married the former Beulah Larsen in 1947.

•BURTON, JOHN L. - U.S. representative from California, was raised and educated in San Francisco public schools. He received a B.A. degree from San Francisco State in 1954 and an LL.B from the University of San Francisco Law School in 1960. He served in the United States Army from 1954 to 1956 and was a member of the California State Assembly from 1965 to 1974. The last four years in the assembly, he served as chairman of the Rules Committee. He was also the sponsor of a state constitutional admendment for open legislative meetings. He led the first successful veto override in California in twenty-eight years to maintain hopitals for the mentally ill and mentally retarded. He was the recipient of the California Society for Autistic Children Award. Chairman of the California Democratic Party from 1973 to 1974, he was elected to the Ninety-third Congress in a special election on June 4, 1974. Reelected four times, he left office at the end of the Ninety-seventh Congress.

•CHAPPIE, EUGENE A. (1920-) - U.S. congressman from California, was born in Sacramento, California, and attended public schools there. He graduated from Sacramento High School in 1938 and was a captain in the United States Army Armored Force South Pacific Service, serving in World War II and the Korean Conflict. A rancher, he was an El Dorado County Supervisor from 1950 to 1964 and a member of the California state legislature from 1964 until 1981. Elected to the Ninety-seventh Congress in 1980, he was reelected two years later. He married Paula Di Benedetto in 1941.

•BURTON, PHILLIP, (1926-1983) - U.S. congressman from California, was born in Cincinnati, Ohio, and moved to San Francisco with his parents in 1939. He attended the public schools of Cincinnati and San Francisco before graduating in political science from the University of Southern California with a B.A. in 1947. Five years later, he received an LL.B from the Golden Gate Law School, was admitted to the state bar, and began practicing law. In 1956, he was admitted to practice before the United States Supreme Court. That same year, he became a member of the state assembly, a position he held until 1964. In 1959, he represented the United States at the Atlantic Treaty Association Conference in France. Elected as a Democrat to the Eighty-eighth Congress to fill the vacancy caused by the resignation of John Shelley. For more than twenty years he lead a liberal-labor coalition that dominated San Francisco politics. He remained in Congress until his death in April, 1983. Two months later, Burton's wife of thirty years, Sala Burton, won a special election to fill the congressman's vacant seat. Burton was a veteran of World War II and the Korean conflict, serving in the U.S. Air Force. He was discharged as a first lieutenant.

•BUTTERFIELD, JOHN, (1801-1869) - expressman and financier, was born in Berne, New York, to Daniel Butterfield, and received his early education in the public schools. In 1822, he moved to Utica to become assistant manager and later manager of a mail stage line between Albanyand Buffalo. He acquired ownership of several stage coach lines in central New York and of a line of steamers plying Lake Ontario and the St. Lawrence river. In 1849, he organized the firm of Butterfield, Wasson & Co., an express business. The following year the company was consolidated with Livingston & Fargo and Wells & Co. to form the American Express Co, which became one of the largest businesses of its kind in the United States. In 1857, the American Express Co. was awarded a $600,000 contract by congress to operate the first transcontinental stage line. Starting in St. Louis, Missouri, the line covered more than 2800 miles as it ran through El Paso, Tucson and Los Angeles to San Francisco. Coaches made the trip twice a week on a running time of twenty-five days. Butterfield joined with Wells, Livingston and others in organizing the New York, Albany and Buffalo Telegraph Co. In 1858, after obtained a contract to carry the mail between San Francisco and the Missouri River, he organized the Butterfield Overland Mail. Under contract with Cornelius Vanderbilt, he inaugurated a mail and passenger service across Nicaragua in 1850. Later, he was identified with the organization and construction of the Utica and Black River railroad, and was manager of the Western Union Telegraph line until his death. He built the Buttterfield house and Butterfield block in Utica, was mayor of the city in 1865, and director of the Utica National Bank. Butterfield married Malinde Harriet Baker in 1822. He died in Utica, N.Y.

C

•CABRILLO, JUAN RODRIGUEZ, (d. 1543) - explorer, was a Portuguese sailor who is credited with the first sighting of Upper California by the sea, and recording the name "California" in his ship journal for the first time. He participated in Cortes' conquest of Mexico, and was then ordered by Viceroy Antonia de Mendoza to look for the mythical Strait of Anian, a projected water route to Asia which was later called the Northwest Passage by English explorers. In his search upon two wretchedly-provisioned ships, he anchored first at what is now the San Diego harbor after leaving Navidad, Mexico in 1542. He went on to visit Catalina Island, San Pedro, Santa Monica, and then Ventura and several other points along the Santa Barbara channel. At next harboring, on San Miguel Island, Cabrillo fell and broke his arm but he insisted on continuing the voyage. Powerful northwest winds and heavy seas prevented the ships from harboring anywhere north of Point Conception and when the little expedition turned around back to San Miguel, Cabrillo died, presumably from an infection resulting from the arm injury. Although his sailors named the island for him at that time, a later explorer named Vizcaino renamed it San Miguel.

In the face of the sea's hardships, Cabrillo's men decided to carry out his dying wish for them to proceed northward, and pilot Bartolome Ferrelo sailed to the present California-Oregon border but could find no new anchorages. The crew was forced three months later to return to Navidad in starving and weakened condition, disappointed at not finding rich cities or straits, and not realizing the importance of their discovery.

A national monument was established at the probable site of Cabrillo's finding landing.

•CABRILLO, JUAN RODRIGUEZ, (d. 1543) - explorer, was a Portuguese sailor who is credited with the first sighting of Upper California by the sea, and recording the name "California" in his ship journal for the first time. He participated in Cortes' conquest of Mexico, and was then ordered by Viceroy Antonia de Mendoza to look for the mythical Strait of Anian, a projected water route to Asia which was later called the Northwest Passage by English explorers. In his search upon two wretchedly-provisioned ships, he anchored first at what is now the San Diego harbor after leaving Navidad, Mexico in 1542. He went on to visit Catalina Island, San Pedro, Santa Monica, and then Ventura and several other points along the Santa Barbara channel. At next harboring, on San Miguel Island, Cabrillo fell and broke his arm but he insisted on continuing the voyage. Powerful northwest winds and heavy seas prevented the ships from harboring anywhere north of Point Conception and when the little expedition turned around back to San Miguel, Cabrillo died, presumably from an infection resulting from the arm injury. Although his sailors named the island for him at that time, a later explorer named Vizcaino renamed it San Miguel.

In the face of the sea's hardships, Cabrillo's men decided to carry out his dying wish for them to proceed northward, and pilot Bartolome Ferrelo sailed to the present California-Oregon border but could find no new anchorages. The crew was forced three months later to return to Navidad in starving and weakened condition, disappointed at not finding rich cities or straits, and not realizing the importance of their discovery.

A national monument was established at the probable site of Cabrillo's finding landing.

•CAMERON, RONALD BROOKS, (1927-1970) - U.S. congressman from California, was born in Kansas City, Missouri, and was educated in the public schools of Missouri, Kansas, and Ohio before entering the Western Reserve Academy, where he remained from 1942 to 1945. During World War Two, he served in the United States Marine Corps. In 1946 he entered the Western Reserve University in Cleveland, Ohio. He attended the University of California, Los Angeles, from 1949 to 1953, and was later admitted to practice as certified public accountant. Elected to the state assembly in 1958 and reelected two years later, Cameron was a delegate to the Democratic National Conventions in 1960 and 1964. He was elected as a Democrat to the Eighty-eighth Congress in 1962, was reelected two years later, and lost a reelection bid in 1966. Stepping down from office in 1967, he returned to his accounting interests. He was a Democratic nominee for State Controller in 1970.

•CAMINETTI, ANTHONY, (1854-1923) - U.S. congressman from California, was born in Jackson, California, and attended the public schools there and in San Francisco, before attending the University of California at Berkeley. After studying law, he was admitted to the bar in 1877 and began practicing in his native city. From 1878 to 1882, he was district attorney of Amador County, and in 1880, he was the Democratic alternate elector for the second congressional district. Caminetti served in the state asembly from 1883 to 1885 and in the state senate from 1885 to 1887. The following year he was a Democratic presidential elector on the Cleveland and Thurman ticket. In 1890, he was elected as a Democrat to the Fifty-first Congress, becoming the first native citizen of California to be elected to Congress. Reelected two years later, he was defeated in a reelection bid in 1894. He was a delegate to the Democratic National Convention at Chicago in 1896, and was again a member of the state assembly from 1896 to 1900. In 1897, he was appointed code commissioner and served in that capacity until 1899. Later, he was a member of the state senate (1907-1913), a Democratic presidential elector on the Wilson and Marshall ticket (1912), and a United States commissioner of immigration (1913-1921). When war was declared with Germany in 1917, he was appointed a member of the War Industries Board, and after the war, he was sent to Europe to investigate conditions there. He eventually returned to his law practice in Jackson, where he remained until his death there in 1923.

•CANNON, MARION, (1834-1920) - U.S. congressman from California, was born in Morgantown, Virginia (now West Virginia), and was trained as a blacksmith. He moved to California in 1852 and worked as a miner in Nevada County for twenty-one years. In 1869, he was elected county recorder of Nevada County. He served for two years and then moved to Ventura County, where he became involved in agriculture. Cannon was elected as the first state president of the Farmers' Allicance in 1890. He was reelected to that position in 1891, the same year that he organized the People's Party of California and that he served as a representative to the supreme counil in Indianapolis. He was selected by the council to represent the state of California in the industrial conference at St. Louis in 1892. Later that year, he served as chairman of the People's Party National Convention at Omaha. In 1892, he was elected as the candidate of the People's and Democratic parties to the Fifty-third Congress. He was not a candidate for reelection two years later. Leaving office in 1895, he continued his agricultural pursuits in Ventura until his death there several years later.

•CAPTAIN JACK, (c.1837-1873) - leader of Modoc Indians. Although his Modoc name was Kintpuash or "having the water brash," he was called "Captain Jack" by the whites because of the military ornaments he wore. In 1872, the United States government tried to force the Modocs to move to a reservation in Klamath. A battle ensued, and the Indians escaped to the lava beds near Tule Lake, California. For several weeks, the American army tried unsuccessfully to dislodge them from the stronghold. In April of 1873, Gen. Edward Canby and two of his officers met with Captain Jack and his followers to negotiate a peace treaty. At a prearranged signal the Indians killed all the commmmissioners, and then quickly returned to the lava beds. Under the command of Col. Jefferson Davis, a force of more than a thousand soldiers finally drove the 80 Indian warriors and their families from their stronghold. Among those taken captive, Captain Jack and three of his subordinates were subsequently executed.

•**CARMANY, JOHN H.**, (1840-1910) - publisher, was born in Pennsylvania, but moved to California in 1858 to become a miner. When that proved unsuccessful, he became a printer, which had been his original profession, and in 1869 he bought the *Overland Monthly*, a one-year-old publication, from Anton Roman. Carmany tried to hold Bret Harte as editor, but Harte resigned in 1871 to return to the east. Soon, the publication began to lose money and Carmany sold it in 1875.

•**CARRILLO** - a prominent California family which began its ranchero and political holdings when Jose Raimundo Carrillo came from Loreto with Portola in 1769. The descendents of this man gained a 300,000-acre estate and became part of the power force of the southern part of the state's politics. Jose's daughter Maria married Jose de la Guerra, and one of his sons, Carolos Antonio bought Rancho Sespe and was appointed governor of California (1837-38), although he was unsuccessful in office against Alvarado and his men. Another son, Jose Antonio, was aligned with Pio Pico and others in the south in a revolt against *norteno* Governor Victoria in 1831.

Jose defended Mexico and held off American troops in the battle to seize Los Angeles, but soon after, he capitulated and signed the Treaty of Cahuenga. His brother Carlos married Maria Josefa Castro, daughter of the great landowner, and Jose himself married two sisters of Pio Pico in succession. Carlos' son Juan Jose became the first mayor of Santa Monica, and one of his daughters married William G. Dana, a relative of Richard Henry. Juan Jose's son Leo (1880-1961) starred in Hollywood films as a partner of the Cisco kid, in which role he glorified the romantic tradition of early California.

Another member of the early family, Joaquin, came to California from Loreto after 1800, and was the father of twelve children who made strategic marriages. Daughter Josepha wed Henry D. Fitch, and American sea captain, and Francisca Benicia wed Gen. Mariano Vallejo. Francisca had two daughters who married sons of Agoston Haraszthy.

Other descendants married into the Vallejo and Castro families as well. Joaquin's daughter Ramona (1811-85) married ffmualdo Pacheco, and was the mother to the younger Ramualdo who became governor of California in 1875.

•CARSON, CHRISTOPHER, (1809-1868) - scout and soldier, was born in Madison County, Kentucky. He was known as Kit Carson. His family moved to Howard County, Missouri, while he was an infant. When he was fifteen he was apprenticed to a saddler, but two years later joined an overland trading expedition to Santa Fe, and became a trapper, roaming over the plains between the Rocky Mountains and the Pacific Ocean. For sixteen years, he lived off the game he shot, and by fur trading. When his Indian wife died in 1842, he brought his daughter to St. Louis, Missouri, to be educated. He sooned joined Lieutenant John C. Fremont on the lieutenant's first expedition to the Rockies. The next year, Carson resumed hunting and trapping after marrying Spanish woman in New Mexico. He joined Fremont's second expedition westward a few years later, and continued with him during the conquest of California in 1846 and 1847. He settled in New Mexico in 1853, and later drove a flock of sheep over the mountains to California, where they commanded a high price because of their scarcity. He returned to Taos, New Mexico, and was appointed U.S. Indian agent for the district. Because of his famaliarity with Indian customs, Carson succeeded in negotiating several important treaties while in that post. During the civil war, he help the union army in the west, and was brevetted brigadier general. When the war ended, he returned to his post as Indian agent. In 1868, he brought a party of Indians to Washington, D.C. He died at Fort Lyon, Colorado.

•CARTER, ALBERT EDWARD, (1881-1964) - U.S. congressman from California, was born in Lemoncove, California, and graduated from San Jose State Normal School in 1903. He school for six years and then was graduated from the law department of the University of California at Berkeleyin 1913. Admitted to the bar the same year, he began practicing in Oakland. From 1917 to

1919, he was a representative of the United States War Department Commission on Training Camps, and from 1920 to 1921, he was an attorney for the California State Board of Pharmacy. Carter served as commissioner of public works of Oakland from 1921 to 1925. As commissioner, he initiated the plan in 1923 for a comprehensive development of the harbor on the east side of San Francsico Bay. He was elected as a Republican to the Sixty-ninth Congress in 1924 and served continuously to 1945, when he was defeated in a bid for an eleventh term. After leaving office, he resumed practicing law in California and Washington, D.C. He died in Oakland.

•CASSERLY, EUGENE, (1822-1883) - senator, was born in Ireland, and was brought to this country by his parents in 1824. He father was a teacher, providing the younger Casserly with an excellent education early education. He graduated from Georgetown College in the District of Columbia, and studied law with a New York lawyer. After working as a corporate lawyer from 1846 to 1847, he moved to San Francisco, and established a practice there. He became active in Democratic politics, and was the editor of a local paper for a time. He was elected state printer, but when his equipment was destroyed by a fire, he was compelled to leave journalism. He was elected to the U.S. senate in 1869, but was forced to resign four years later because of failing health. Returning to his law practice, he remained in San Francisco until his death there ten years later.

•CASTLE, CURTIS HARVEY, (1848-1928) - U.S. congressman from California, was born in Galesburg, Illinois, and was graduated from Northwest University in 1872. He served as prinicpal of the Washington, Texas, public schools from 1872 to 1876. In 1878, he was graduated from the College of Physicians and Surgeons in Keokuk, Iowa. He practiced briefly in Fulton County, Illinois, and in Wayland, Iowa, until 1882, when he moved to Point Arena, California. Six years later he moved to Merced County. From 1894 to 1896, he was a member of the American Academy of Medicine, chairman of the Populist executive committee of Merced, and a member of the state executive committee. He was elected as the candidate of the Populist and Democratic parties to the Fifty-fifth Congress in 1896, but lost a reelection bid two years later. Leaving office in 1899, he resumed his practice in Merced. He retired from active practice in 1915 until the start of the First World War. When the war ended, he again retired, and then moved to Santa Barbara, where he lived until his death there several years later.

•CHAFFEY, GEORGE, (1848-1932) - entrepeneur, was a self-educated engineering genius from Canada. He moved to California in 1880 and after studying irrigation in Riverside, he and his brother William created their idea of ideal communities in Ontario and Etiwanda in San Bernardino County. There, George developed the ideal of mutual water companies with a share of company stock attached to each acre of land. The towns were agricultural, and built on once-barren lands which the brothers irrigated. George founded an agricultural college and the first commercial hydroelectrical plant in California near these towns.

Chaffey's greatest achievement, however, was his establishment of irrigation in the dry lower Colorado River area of the state. The project turned a desert into rich agricultural and residential land, known today as the Imperial Valley. Chaffey had designed the canals that stretched 700 miles through Mexican territory and entering California at two border townsites, which the engineer named Mexicali and Calexico. However, after Chaffey left the company which funded the canal project, his successors built a risky bypass canal around the head gate, and torrential rains caused the river to burst through and flood an Imperial Valley waterbed, creating the Salton Sea.

His surname is sometimes spelled Chaffee.

•CHANDLER, HARRY, (1864-1944) - newspaper publisher, was born in Landaff, New Hampshire, to Moses Knight and Emma Jane Chandler, and attended Dartmouth College. When his health began failing while still a student, he moved in 1885 to Los Angeles, California, where he purchased the Los Angeles Times's circulation routes. Over the years, Chandler rose in importance in the paper, rising to the level president and general manager of the Times-Mirror Company when Harrison G. Otis died in 1917. In 1941, he became chairman of the Times's board of directors, a position he retained until his death. During his time with the paper, Chandler watched the Times grow not just in size and circulation, but in political power. Chandler founded the Colorado River Land Co. in 1899. He then purchased nearly 900,00 acres of land in Mexico for growing cotton. Shortly after the turn of the century, he was an active participant in the construction of the Los Angeles aqueduct, an ambitious and controversial project to channel the water from Owens Valley to Los Angeles. A vast landowner, he also served as a major officer on numerous California corporations. He was a trustee of Stanford University for twenty years, and California Institute of Technology for twenty-five. He married Magdalena Schlador in 1888. She died four years later, and Chandler married Marian Otis in 1894. Otis was the daughter of the Times publisher. Chandler died in Los Angeles.

•CHAPMAN, CHARLES EDWARD, (1880-) - author, was born in Franklin, New Hampshire, to Frank Hilton and Ella Frances James Chapman. His father was a druggist and a member of the New Hampshire legislature. The younger Chapman studied at Princeton University from 1898 to 1900, and graduated from Tufts College in 1902 and Harvard Law School in 1905. The University of California conferred upon him the honorary degree of M.A. in 1909 and that of Ph.D in 1915. From 1912 to 1914, he was engaged in historical research in the Spain while pursuing post-graduate studies at the University of Seville. In 1906, he was admitted to the bar in California and Massachuisetts, and became a special investigator for the United Railways Co. of San Francisco. From 1907 to 1908, he was employed by the Western Electric Co. During the end of the latter year, he forsook law, to begin pursuing teaching and writing. His first teaching assignment was at the Riverside (California) High School, where he taught history from 1909 to 1910. From there he went to the University of California as assistant in history, becoming an instructor upon his return from Spain in 1914. He was advanced to assistant professor in 1915 and associate professor in 1919. In 1920, he was an American Exhange professor to Chile. As an author he concentrated on the Spanish history of both Americas. His books are *The Founding of Spanish California* (1916), *A California in South America* (1917), *A History of Spain* (1918), *Catalogue of Material in the Archivo General de Indias for the Hisotry of the Pacific Coast and the American Southwest* (1919), and *A History of California: the Spanish Period* (1921). During 1917-19, he was one of the eidotrs on the active board of the *Hispanic-American Historical Review* and in 1921 he became an advisory editor of the publication.

•CHAVEZ, CESAR, (1927-) - labor leader, was born in Brawley, California, and worked much of his chilhood as a migrant farm laborer, which made it difficult to obtain his eight years of formal education.

He served in the navy and then became active in union organizations and Mexican-American community service before beginning the task of organizing a union called the National Farm Workers Association in 1962. Although the new union was independent of the AFL-CIO Agricultural Workers Organizing Committee because Chavez saw the NFWA members as well-organized crews working with no-strike contracts, he decided to join the larger organization in 1965 to strike against 33 grape growers in Kern County. In 1966, after a series of victories for the unions that led to more large scale unionization of farms across the state, Chavez' NFWA and the AOC merged to form the UFW, or the United Farm Workers organizing committee. The months-long strike was marked by dramatic and even religious fervor as Chavez and his followers walked a symbolic 300-mile march from Delano to Sacramento, and later observed a 25-day fast. Increasing sympathy on the part of the public for the minority workers' plight helped bring victory for them out of the strike, as many supported a boycott of table grapes at that time. The grape strike and a later UFW lettuce pickers strike placed Chavez' union as one of the most influential in the country, and marked a social movement for equal rights and fairer working conditions for minorities.

Chavez gained the respect of many in governmental positions, and Robert Kennedy espoused the UFW cause in 1968 during his presidential primary campaigning. Governor "Jerry" Brown chose Chavez as the only man to nominate him for President in the 1976 Democratic National Convention. In 1977, the Teamsters Union signed an agreement with Chavez to grant the UFW the exclusive right to represent field workers, while other workers would be represented by the Teamsters.

•CHEN, THEODORE HSE-EN, (1902-) - educator, was born in Foochow, China, and received an A.B. degree from Fekien Christian University in 1922, an A.M. from Columbia University in 1929, and a Ph.D from University of Southern California in 1939. After receving his M.A., he was appointed dean of faculty at the Fukien University, a post he held until 1938, when he was hired as a professor of Asian Studies at USC. In 1974, he was named professor emeritus. Over the years, Chen has published numerous articles in professional journals and several books in his field of study. His published books include, *Thought Reform of Chinese Intellectuals, Teacher Training in Communist China, Developing Patterns of the College Curriculum in the United States, Chinese Communism and the Socialist-Proletarian Revolution.* He married Wen-Hui Chung in 1932.

•CHICAGO, JUDY, (1939-) - artist, was born in Chicago, Illinois, to Arthur M. Cohen, a union organizer, and May Levenson Cohen, a medical secretary. She studied at the University of California, Los Angeles, where she attained her B.A. in 1962 and her M.A. in 1964.

A multi-talented, artist, writer and teacher, she was an assistant professor, starting the first women's art program at California State University (1969-71). She was a faculty member and co-founder of the feminist art program at the California Institute of the Arts (1971-73), and the founder/instructor of the Feminist Studio Workshop in Los Angeles (1973-74).

From 1975 to 1979, Judy Chicago worked on the major museum exhibition entitled the *Dinner Party.* The *Dinner Party* covers 1,000 square feet. It consists of a triangular table with 39 place settings, situated on a 2300-tile floor. Each hand-crafted porcelain plate and its accompanying hand-sewn cloth runner depicts a woman important for her part in the different phases of history. The tile floor is inscribed with the names of 999 additional significant women, names spanning the myths of the past, to the present. This work of art traveled around the country in 1979 and 1980, opening at the San Francisco Museum of Modern Art, March to June, 1979. In 1971, she joined with artist Miriam Shapiro and they established the Feminist Art Program at the California Institute of the Arts, Valencia. In 1972 the class created *Womanhouse*, a display of feminine fantasies about domestic interiors, from a dilapitated old mansion in Los Angeles. It attracted 10,000 visitors when it was opened for a month to the public during that year. In 1973, *Womanspace*, an exhibition space and art gallery, sprang from a nationwide conference for women artists that Judy Chicago had organized at Cal Arts the year before. In 1973, along with Arlene Raven, art historian, and Sheila de Bretteville, designer, she founded the Feminist Studio Workshop, committed to sharpening leadership and art skills. From this they established Woman's Building, an alternative arts institution, in Los Angeles in 1974.

Married twice, her first, to Jerry Gerowitz in 1961, ended with his death in an automobile accident in 1963. Her marriage to sculptor Lloyd Hamrol in 1969 ended in divorce in 1979. Born Judy Cohen, she changed her name to Judy Chicago in 1970 as a statement of her independence from "male social dominance."

•CHURCH, DENVER SAMUEL, (1862-1952) - U.S. congressman from California, was born in Folsom City, California, and graduated from Healdsburg College in 1885. After studying law, he was admitted to the bar in 1893 and commenced practicing in Fresno. Church served as district attorney of Fresno County from 1907 until 1913, when he was elected as a Democrat to the Sixty-third Congress. Reelected twice, Church was a delegate to the Democratic National Convention in St. Louis in 1916. He was not a candidate for renomination in 1918. When his final term expired in 1919, he returned to his law practice. Church became a superior judge of Fresno County in 1924 and served in that capacity until 1930. In 1932 he was again elected to Congress. Two years later he did not seek renomination, and when his term expired in 1935, he returned to his law practice. He died in Fresno.

•CLAUSEN, DON H. - U. S. representative from California, was born, raised and attended public schools in Humboldt County, California. He was the son of Marie S. and Henry A. Clausen. He attended San Jose College, California Polytechnic, Weber State College in Utah, and St. Mary's College in California, and holds honorary degrees of LL.D. from Pacific Union College, California, and AL.D. from Embry Riddle Aeronautical University, Florida.

A U.S. Navy piot in World War II, he married Ollie Piper. He has been in banking, insurance, and professional aviation. His government service includes 7 years as Del Norte, California supervisor. He is also past president, Supervisors Unit, Redwood Empire Association, and past chairman, California Aerospace-Aviation Education Task Force. He was the 1978 winner of Frank G. Brewer Trophy, the nation's highest award for aerospace education. Elected to the 88th Congress, in a special election, January 22, 1963, he remained in office through the end of the Ninety-seventh Congress. A Republican, he was the ranking minority member during his final term in Congress.

•CLAWSON, DELWIN MORGAN (1914-) - U.S. representative from California, was born in Thatcher, Arizona, and was educated in Pima and Safford, Arizona, public schools. He attended Gila College in Thatcher. He was employed as a salesman and bookkeeper from 1934 until 1941, when he began working for the United States Employment Service and Federal Public Housing Authority. He left that position in 1947 to become manager of the Mutual Housing Association of Compton. A member of Compton's Park and Recreation Commission from 1950 to 1953 and of the city council from 1953 to 1953, he became mayor of Compton in 1957, and remained in that position until 1963, when he was elected as a Republican to the Eighty-eighth Congress. He was reelected to each succeeding Congress through the Ninety-fifth Congress. He retired from office in 1979. He married the former Marjorie Anderson in 1934.

•CLAYTON, CHARLES, (1825-1885) - U.S. congressman from California, was born in Devonshire, England, and immigrated in 1842 to the United States, where he settled in Wisconsin. He moved to Oregon in 1847 and to San Francisco the following year. In 1849 and 1850, he was alcalde of Santa Clara, and two years later, he built the Santa Clara flour mills. He returned to San Francisco in 1853 and became engaged in the grain and flour business. He was a member of the state assembly from 1863 to 1866 and the San Francisco board of supervisors from 1864 to 1869. He was appointed surveyor of customs of the port and district of San Francisco by President Grant in 1870. Two years later, he was elected as a Republican to the Forty-third Congress. After serving one term, he did not seek renomination. Later, he served as state prison director (1881-1882). He died in Oakland.

•CLUNIE, THOMAS JEFFERSON, (1852-1913) - U.S. congressman from California, was born in St. John's, New Foundland, while his parent were on a vist there from Massachusetts. He moved with his parents to California in 1854, but later returned to east coast and settled in Maine. In 1861, he returned to California, where he attended the public schools. After studying law, he was admitted to the bar in 1868. Two years later, he commenced practicing in Sacramento. In 1875, Clunie was a member of the state assembly, and in 1884, he was a delegate to the Democratic National Convention of Chicago. He served in the state senate from 1887 to 1889, when he began serving his only term in Congress. Two years later, he was defeated in a reelection bid. When his term expired, Clunie returned to his law practice. He died in San Francisco. In addition to his professional work, he took an active part in the state militia and was retired as brigadier general.

•COELHO, TONY (1942-) - U.S. representative from California, was born in Los Banos, California, and graduated for Dos Palos High School in 1960. He received a B.A. from Loyola University in Los Angeles in 1964. At on point, he was an administrative assistant to United States Congressman B.F. Sisk. Elected as a Democrat to the Ninety-Sixth Congress in 1978, he was reelected in 1980 and 1982.

•COFFMAN, L. DALE, (1905-) - lawyer and educator, was born in Delta, Iowa, to Ralph Gideon and Georgia Green Coffman and received his B.A. (1926) and J.D. (1928) from University of Iowa. He also received an LL.M (1929) and an S.J.D. (1935) from Harvard University. Admitted to practice law in Iowa (1928), New York (1938) and Tennessee (1946), Coffman was hired as a professor of law at University of Nebraska in 1931. He remained in that position until 1937, when he became counsel for the General Electric Company. Nine years later he left General Electric to become dean of Vanderbilt University Law School. In 1949 he was appointed dean of the law school at the University of California, Los Angeles, and from 1957 to 1973, Coffman worked as a professor of law at the university. Then in 1973, he was made professor emeritus. A member of the American Judicature Society, Seldon Society, and the American Bar Association, he has written numerous articles for professional journals. He married Helen Crouch in 1925.

•COGHLAN, JOHN MAXWELL, (1835-1895) - U.S. congressman from California, was born in Louisville, Kentucky, and moved with his parents to Illinois in 1847. Three years later, his family moved to California and settled in Suisun city. After studying law, he was admitted to the state bar and began practicing in Suisun. A member of the state assembly in 1865 and 1966, he was elected as a Republican to the Forty-second Congress in 1870. Two years later, he was defeated in a reelection bid. When his term expired in 1873, he returned to his law practice. He died in Oakland.

•COHELAN, JEFFERY, (1914-) - U.S. congressman from California, was born in San Francisco, California, and graduated with an A.B. from the University of California School of Economics. He was secretary-treasurer of the Milk Drivers and Dairy Employees Union, Local 302, of Alameda and Contra Costa counties from 1942 until 1958, when he was elected as a Democrat to the Eight-sixth Congress. From 1849 to 1953, he was a member of the Berkeley Welfare Commission. The following two years, Cohelan was a Fulbright research scholar at Leeds and Oxford Universities in England. After returning home, he served on the Berkeley City Council from 1955 to 1958, the year he was elected to Congress. He remained in Congress for six consecutive terms, but was then defeated in a reelection bid in 1970. Later, he was the executive director of the Group Health Association of America.

•COLE, CORNELIUS, (1822-1924) - U. S. Senator and congressman from California, was born in Lodi, Seneca County, New York and attended the common schools, Ovid Academy at Ovid, Lima Seminary at Lima, and Hobart College at Geneva, N.Y. He graduated from Wesleyan University in Middletown, Connecticut, in 1847. After Studying law, he was admitted to the bar in Auburn, New York in 1848. He went to California in 1849, and after working a year in the gold mines commenced the practice of law in San Francisco in 1850. Cole moved to Sacramento in 1851. He served as district attorney of Sacramento City and County from 1859 to 1862, and as a member of the republican National Committee from 1856-1860, before moving to Santa Cruz in 1862. During the Civil War, Cole was commissioned as a captain in the Union Army in 1863, the same year that he was elected as a Union Republican to the Thirty-eighth Congress. He served from 1963 to 1965. Two years later, he was elected to the United States Senate and served from 1867 to 1873, when he left office to resume the practice of law.

He moved to Colegrove, Los Angeles County, California in 1880, and retired from active practice. When he had nearly attained one hundred years of age he came to Washington, D. C., and visited the Capitol, and during a recess of five minutes taken for that purpose by the House of Representatives he addressed that body in 1922. He died in Hollywood.

•COLELMAN, WILLIAM TELL, (1824-1893) - pioneer and merchant, was born in Harrison County, Kentucky to Napoleon B. Coleman, a prominent attorney. Educated in the public schools, he began work as a surveyor in an uncle's company. He later moved to St. Louis, where he engaged in the lumber business. At eighteen, he entered St. Louis University. He graduated from there after completing the usual four-year program in two years. Shortly afterwards, he returned to the lumber business and remained there until 1949, when he followed the tide of gold-seekers to California, where he established a small carpentering and building business in Sacramento. Within a year, he moved to San Francisco and set up a business as a shipping and commission merchant. His business grew so well that by 1952 he had opened a branch in New York. Four years later, he introduced a shipping line between those two cities. As his business grew, Coleman became active in civic affairs, serving as president of the state's vigilance committees of 1852 and 1856. At the close of the civil War, he conceived a plan of organized assistance for the destitute in the South, which he put into operation with the help of Horace Greeley and Henry Ward Beecher. Later, he projected an addition to the town of San Rafael with thirty-four miles of streets. At one time, his firm controlled the fruit canning industry in California.

   In 1852, Coleman married Carrie Page, the daughter of a prominent St. Louis banker. Coleman died in San Francisco.

•COLLINS, SAMUEL LAFORT, (1895-1965) - U.S. congressman from California, was born in Fortville, Hancock County, Indiana, and attended the public schools of Indiana and California, before graduating from Chaffey Union High School of Ontario, in 1915.

   He enlisted as a private in the Hospital Corps, Seventh Infantry, California National Guard, in 1916, served on the Mexican border, and was discharged a few months later. During the First World War he served in the United States Army from 1917, to 1919 as a sergeant in Company C, Three Hundred and Sixty-fourth Infantry, Ninety-first Division.

   After studying law, he was admitted to the bar in 1921 and commenced practice in Fullerton, California. He served as assistant district attorney of Orange County from 1926 to 1930 and district attorney from 1930 to 1932, when he was elected as a Republican to the Seventy-third Congress. Reelected two years later, he was an unsuccessful candidate for reelection in 1936 to the Seventy-fifth Congress. He was a member of the State assembly from 1940 to 1952, serving as speaker for the last five years. In 1952, he resumed the practice of law. He died in Fullerton.

•COLTON, WALTER, (1797-1851) - writer and newspaper publisher, was born in Rutland, Vermont, and graduated from Yale College (1822). He taught for a time, and then entered Andover Theological Seminary. In 1825, he was appointed chair of moral philosophy and belles-lettres at the Middletown Academy in Connecticut, a post he retained until 1828, when he moved to Washington, D.C., to edit the "American Spectator." He was made a chaplain in the navy by Pres. Andrew Jackson, and served on the Vincennes in the West Indies and the Constellation in the Mediterranean. Later, he was stationed in Charlestown, Mass., where he edited the "Colonization Herald." He was transferred to Philadephia in 1838 and was named editor of the "North American" three years later. In the early 1840s, he wrote "The Bible - the Public School." A few years before the war with Mexico began, Colton was sent to California and made alcalde of Monterey. Here he established "California," the first newspaper published in California. When he moved to San Francisco a short time later, Colton brought the paper with him, changing the name to "Alta California." He also is credited with building the first school house on the coast,and with making the first public announcement of the discovery of gold by a letter in the columns of the "North American." He remained in California until 1849, when he returned to Philadelphia. He lived there until his death. Among the books he wrote are "Ship and Shore in Madeira, Lisbon and the Mediterranean" (1835); "A Visit to Athens and Constantinople" (1836); "Three Years in California" (1850); and "Deck and Port" (1850).

•CONDON, ROBERT LIKENS, (1912-) - U.S. congressman from California, was born in Berkeley, California and attended the public schools. He graduated from the University of California at Berkeley in 1934 and from the law college of the same university in 1938, the same year that he was editor in chief of the California Law Review, admitted to the California bar and was hired as an attorney for National Labor Relations Board. He left the labor Board in 1942 to join the Office of Price Administration as chief enforcement attorney for northern California. He later was regional investigator for five Western States.

He entered the United States Army as a private in December 1942 and served overseas in the European Theater with Company G, Three Hundred and Tenth Infantry Regiment, Seventy-eighth Division, in France, Belgium, and Germany. Discharged in February 1946 as a staff sergeant he was decorated with two battle stars and the Silver Star.

Condon engaged in private practice of law in 1946 in Martinez, California and served in the California State Assembly from 1948 to 1952, when he was elected as a Democrat to the Eighty-third Congress. An unsuccessful candidate for reelection in 1954 to the Eighty-fourth Congress, he resumed law practice in Martinez.

•CONNESS, JOHN, (1821-1909) - U.S. senator, was born in Abbey, County Calaway, Ireland, and immigrated to the United States in 1833. He learnerd the art of pianoforte making in New York before moving to California in 1840 to engage in mining and mercantile pursuits. He served as a member of the State assembly in 1853-1854, 1860 and 1861. He was an unsuccessful candidate for governor of California in 1861, but was elected as a Douglass Democrat (afterwards changed to a Union Republican) to the United States Senate and served from 1863 to 1869.

He moved to Boston, Massachusetts in 1869 and retired from active business pursuits. He died in Jamaica Plain, Massachusetts.

•COOMBS, FRANK LESLIE, (1853-1934) - U.S. representative from California, was born in Napa, California and attended the public schools there before attending Dorchester High School, Boston, Massachusetts. He graduated from the law department of Columbian (now George Washington) University, Washington, D.C., in 1875 and was admitted to the bar in 1875. He commenced prsotice in Napa, and served as district attorney of Napa County, from 1880 to 1885.

He was a member of the state assembly (1887-1889 and 1891-1897) and served as speaker in 1891 and again in 1897. On the death of John F. Swift, Coombs was appointed United States Minister to Japan and served from 1892 to 1893. He was state librarian of California from 1898, to 1899, and United States attorney for the northern district of California from 1899, to 1901, when he was elected as a Republican to the Fifty-seventh Congress. An unsuccessful candidate for reelection in 1902, he resumed the practice of law in Napa. Again a member of the State assembly 1921-1923 and 1925-1927, he died in Napa.

•COONS, ARTHUR GARDINER, (1900-1968) - educator, was born in Anaheim, California, to Richard LaSalle and Mary Ella Gardiner Coons and received a B.A. from Occidental College (1920), an M.A. from University of Pennsylvania (1922), and a Ph.D from the University of Pennsylvania (1927). In addition, he received numerous honorary degrees. After earning his Ph.D Coons embarked on a career as an educator, first as an instructor of economics and finance, and later as an administrator at a number of colleges and universities. Widely known among educators, Coons was president of Occidental College from 1946 to 1965. Upon retiring he was named president emeritus. In 1956, he was president of the Association of American Colleges, and in 1965 he became president of the Coordinating Council for Higher Education in California. He was the author of numerous articles on economics and education. Married to Edna Palmer in 1927, he died in Newport Beach.

•CORMAN, JAMES CHARLES, (1920-) - U.S. representative from California, was born in Galena, Cherokee County, Kansas and moved with his family in 1933 to Los Angeles, California where he attended the public schools. He graduated from the University of California at Los Angeles in 1942, and from the University of Southern California Law School in 1948.

During World War II, Corman served as a lieutenant in the United States Marine Corps with the Third Marine Division, 1942-1946, and was in the Bougainville, Guam, and Iwo Jima actions. He also served in the United States Marine Corps, 1950-1952.

Admitted to the bar in 1949 he engaged in the practice of law in Van Nuys. He was a member of Los Angeles City Council, 1957-1960, and the President's National Advisory Commission on Civil Disorders, 1967-1968. Elected as a Democrat to the Eighty-seventh Congress, he served from 1961 to 1981.

•COSTELLO, JOHN MARTIN, (1903-) - U.S. representative from California, was born in Los Angeles, California and attended the public schools. He graduated from the law department of Loyola University in Los Angeles in 1924, was admitted to the bar the same year and commenced practice in his home town. A teacher in Los Angeles secondary schools in 1924 and 1925, he was an unsuccessful candidate for election to the Seventy-third Congress in 1932, but was elected as a Democrat to the Seventy-fourth and to the four succeeding Congresses (January 3, 1935-January 3, 1945). He was an unsuccessful candidate for renomination in 1944.

When his final term ended, he worked as general counsel and manager of the Washington office of the Los Angeles Chamber of Commerce (1945-1947) and in the practice of law in Washington, D.C.

•COURTNEY, HOWARD PERRY, (1911-) - clergyman, was born in Frederick, Oklahoma, to C.C. and Dottie Lee Welchel Courtney and graduated from Life Bible College in 1932. He later attended specialized courses at the University of Illinois and Los Angeles City College. A Doctor of Divinity and Doctor of Theology, Courtney joined the International Church of the Foursquare Gospel in Los Angeles, California, in 1953 as vice president, a position he retained until 1973. Since 1953, he has also been pasture of the Angelus Temple in Los Angeles. In 1953 and 1954, he served as chairman of the Pentecostal Fellowship of North America. From 1959 to 1961, he was chairman of the Pentecostal Advisory World Conference. He has also served on the Board of Administration of the National Association of Evangelicals. He is married to the former Vaneda Harper.

•COURVILLE, CYRIL BRIAN, (1900-1968) - neurologist and educator, was born in Traverse City, Michigan, to Philip Albert and Emma Amelia Kroupa Courville and was educated at Emanuel Missionary College, College of Medical Evangelists (M.D. 1925) and at the University of Southern California (M.Sc). He was an honorary professor of neurology at Loma Linda University Medical School and a consultant in Neurology for the Department of Los Angeles County Hospital and Los Angeles Coroners Office. He taught neurology at the Loma Linda University Medical School from 1926 to 1929, when he was promoted to the professorship position, a post he retained until his death. A Lieutenant Colonel in the Medical Reserve Corps, he was a fellow of American Medical Association, American Neurological Association, and American Neurological and Psychiatric Association. He authored some 16 books and monographs, and contributed hundreds of articles to various medical and scientific journals. He married Margaret Farnsworth in 1939.

•CRAIL, JOE, (1877-1938) - U.S. representative from California, was born in Fairfield, Jefferson County, Iowa, and attended the public schools. He graduated from Drake University in Des Moines, Iowa, in 1898.

During the Spanish-American War, he enlisted as a private in the Twelfth Company, United States Volunteer Signal Corps. Promoted to corporal, he served in the American Army of Occupation in Cuba until its withdrawal. After the war, he studied law at Iowa College of Law in Des Moines, was admitted to the bar in 1903 and commenced practice in Fairfield, Iowa. He moved to California in 1913, settled in Los Angeles, and practiced law until elected to Congress. He served as chairman of the Republican state central committee for southern California (1918-1920) and was elected as a Republican to the Seventieth, Seventy-first, and Seventy-second Congresses (March 4, 1927-March 3, 1933). He was not a candidate for renomination in 1932, but was an unsuccessful candidate for nomination as United States Senator.

When his final term ended, he resumed the practice of law, and also engaged in banking. He died in Los Angeles.

•CRANSTON, ALAN, (1914-) - U.S. Senator from California (1968-) and minority whip, is one of the leading contenders for the Democratic nomination for President in 1984. He was born in Palo Alto, California, but moved to the Los Angeles area, where he attended Pomona College in 1932-33. In 1935, he traveled to Mexico city to study at the university there, but the next year he completed studies toward a B.A. degree at Stanford.

Cranston worked as a foreign correspondent for the International News Service in 1936-38, traveling to England, Italy and Ethiopa on assignment. Involved in politics at an early age, Cranston returned to the U.S. in 1939 to work as a lobbyist for the Common Council for American Unity. Soon afterwards, however, he joined the army to serve out World War II.

California began to experience its greatest growth after the war, and Cranston capitalized on this by working in real estate and the building industry in the late 1940s to 1960s. In the meantime he was active in various liberal political groups, including the United World Federalists, and he founded the Democratic Council of California. In 1958 he was elected state controller, serving until 1966. He then continued his business interests until 1968, when he was elected for the first time to the U.S. Senate. Since then, he has been reelected twice. In each of his campaigns, Cranston made the arms race a central issue. He backed the SALT negotiations, and advocated arms reduction in his seat on the foreign relations committee. He also sits on the banking, housing and urban affairs committees in the Senate. Youth has always interested him, and in recent years he has proposed measures to involve more young people in public service, including a plan to revitalize the Peace Corps. Cranston is very popular among his California constituents; in 1980 he became the first U.S. Senator ever to gain over 4 million votes for his reelection.

Some criticize Cranston's age, but at 69 years, he continues to hold the record in the 100-yard dash for his age group. Senator Cranston is known for his quiet persuasiveness on Capitol Hill, but he is making a strong statement on the state of nuclear armaments in his new campaign. He became an early seeker of the presidency in 1983 and campaigned vigorously but withdrew in March, 1984 after poor showings in the early primaries and caucuses.

•CROSTEN, WILLIAM LORAN, (1909-) - musician and educator, was born in Des Moines, Iowa, to Sidney F. and William T. Crosten and was educated at Drake University where he received his B.A. in music, the University of Iowa (M.A.) and Columbia University (Ph.D). From 1942 to 1946, he served in the U.S. Navy and was discharged with the rank of Lt. Commander. He was an associate professor and later a full professor at Stanford University from 1946 to 1973. At the same time, he served as Executive Head of the Department of Music. In 1954, he was awarded a Guggenheim Fellowship, and in 1964, he received the Distinguished Alumnus Award from Drake University and the Steinway Award for Service to Music. A member of the American Musicological Society and the College Music Society, Crosten published *French Grand Opera* and contributed numerous articles and reviews to leading music journals. He is married to Mary E. Perry.

•CURRY, CHARLES FORREST, (1858-1930) - U.S. representative from California, was born in Naperville, Du Page County, Wisconsin, and attended the common schools and the Episcopal

Academy in Mineral Point, Wisconsin. He studied one year at the University of Washington at Seattle, and also was educated by a private tutor. He moved with his parents to Seattle in 1872, and from there to San Francisco, California, in 1873. He was engaged in agricultural pursuits and the cattle, lumber, and mining businesses.

A member of the state assembly in 1887 and 1888, he was admitted to the bar of San Francisco in 1888, and worked as superintendent of Station B post office in San Francisco (1890-1894). Clerk of San Francisco city and county (1894-1898) and secretary of state of California (1899-1910), he was an unsuccessful candidate for the Republican nomination for Governor in 1910. He was appointed building and loan commissioner of California in 1911 and was the representative to the Panama Pacific International Exposition for the Pacific Coast and Intermountain States in 1911. Elected as a Republican to the Sixty-third and to the eight succeeding Congresses, he served from March 4, 1913, until his death in Washington, D.C.

•CUTTING, JOHN TYLER, (1844-1911_ - U.S. representative from California, was born in Westport, Essex County, New York, and was left an orphan at ten years of age, when he journeyed westward and resided in Wisconsin and Illinois from 1855 to 1860, he worked on a farm. While employed as a clerk in a mercantile establishment, he attended the public schools of Illinois.

He enlisted in Taylor's Chicago Battery at the outbreak of the civil War and served until July 20, 1862. Discharged for disability, the result of service in the field, he reenlisted January 4, 1864, in the Chicago Mercantile Battery, in which he served until the close of the war.

He moved to California in 1877 and established a wholesale fruit and commission business. A member of the National Guard of California, he subsequently assisted in the organization of the Coast Guard, of which he later became brigadier general in command of the second Brigade. Elected as a Republican to the Fifty-second Congress (March 4, 1891-March 3, 1893) he declined to be a candidate for renomination in 1892.

He returned to the East in 1894 and settled in New York City, where he became interested in the automobile industry. He retired to his old home in Westport, New York, in 1907. He died in Toronto, Ontario, Canada, where he had gone to recuperate his health.

D

•DAGGETT, MALCOLM DANIEL, (1907-) - educator, was born in Pasadena, California, to Arthur George and Mattie Clare Taylor Daggett and graduated from Bowdoin College (B.A. 1929) and Harvard University (M.A. 1932, Ph.D 1939). He taught briefly at both of his alma maters and at the University of Rochester before he was hired as a professor of Romance languages at the University of Vermont in 1945. From 1945 to 1967, he was chairman of the university's Romance language department. When he retired in 1973, he was named professor emeritus. A member of the American Association of Teachers of French and the Modern Language Association, Daggett was awarded the Chevalier de l'ordre des *Palmes* Academiques by the French government. He married Frances Hutchinson Lintner in 1937.

•DANIELSON, GEORGE E. (1915-) - U.S. representative from California, was born in Wausa, Nebraska, to August and Ida Younger Danielson. He attended the Wausa public schools and Wayne State College, before graduating from tyhe University of Nebraska with a B.A. in 1937 and a J.D. in 1939. After leaving the university, Danielson worked as a special agent for the Federal Bureau of Investigation from 1939 until 1944. During World War II, he was a lieutenant in the United States Naval Reserve. From 1949 to 1951, he was Assistant U.S. Attorney for the Southern District of California. A practicing attorney, he was admitted to practice before the United States Supreme Court in 1955. Elected to the California Assembly in 1962 and 1964, he served until 1966, when he was elected to the state Senate. He was reelected two years later. In 1971, he authored *Cable Antenna Television in California.* Elected to the Ninety-second Congress on November

3, 1970, he was reelected to each succeeding Congress before leaving office at the end of the Ninety-seventh Congress in 1983. He is married to the former Gladys C. Ohanian.

•DANNEMEYER, WILLIAM E. (1929-) - U.S. representative from California, was born in Los Angeles, California, where he attended Trinity Lutheran School, before graduating from Long Beach Poly High School in 1946. He attended Santa Maria Junior College (1946-1947) and graduated from Valparaise University in Indiana (B.A. 1950) and Hastings Law School (J.D. 1952). He served in the United States Army Counter Intelligence Corp from 1952 until 1954. Admitted to the state bar in 1953, he commenced practicing in Santa Barbara in 1955. He was a member of the California Assembly (1963-1966, 1976-1977), deputy district attorney (1955-1957), and assistant city attorney of Fullerton (1959-1962). He has also served as a municipal court judge pro tem (1966-1976) and a superior court judge pro tem (1966-1976). A member of the California state Republican Central Committee, he was elected as a Republican to the Ninety-sixth Congress on November 7, 1978. Reelected in 1980 and 1982, he is a member of the current Ninety-eighth Congress. He married Evelyn Hoemann in 1955.

•DAVIDSON, HAROLD PRESCOTT, (1908-) - educator, was born in in New York, New York, to Dr. and Mrs. H.S. Davidson and was educated at Pomona College (B.A. 1929), Claremont Colleges (M.A. 1932) and the University of Southern California. After a variety of teaching assignments, he wa hired as chairman of the music department at California State Polytechnic College in 1936. He remained in that post until 1973, when he retired. He has been a member of A.S.C.A.P. and the College Music Society. In addition, he has directed several college glee clubs, vocal ensembles and bands. He is also the composer of numerous publshed choral works. He married Rosalie Evelyn Clark in 1959.

•DE VRIES, MARION, (1865-1939) - U. S. representative from California was born on a ranch near Woodbridge, San Joaquin County, California, and attended the public schools. He graduated from the San Joaquin Valley College in 1886 and from the law department of the University of Michigan at Ann Arbor in 1888. Admitted to the bar in 1887, he commenced practice in Stockton, California in 1889.

He was assistant district attorney of San Joaquin County from January 1893 to February 1897, when he resigned, having been elected as a Democrat to the Fifty-fifth Congress. Reelected two years later, he served from March 4, 1897, to August 20, 1900, when he signed to accept an appointment to the Board of General Appraisers (now United States Customs Court) at New York City. He served until his resignation in 1910. He was president of the board the last few years of his term. He was an associate judge of the United States Court of Customs Appeals from April 2, 1910, to June 30, 1921, and served as presiding judge from July 1, 1921, until October 31, 1922, when he resigned. Later, he practiced law in Washington, D.C., and New York City, until 1939, when he retired to his ranch near Woodbridge, where he died later that year.

•DELLUMS, RONALD V. (1935-) - U.S. representative from California, was born in Oakland, California, and was educated at McClymonds High School and Oakland Technical High School. He received an A.A. degree from Oakland City College in 1958, a B.A degree from San Francisco State College in 1960, an M.S.W. from the University of California in 1975, and an honorary doctor of law from Wilberforce University in 1975. He served in the United States Marine Corps for two years and was honorably discharged. Employed in various social service related jobs over the years, he was a psychiatric social worker at the Department of Mental Hygiene (1962-1964), program director of Bayview Community Center (1964-1965), associate director, and later director, of the Hunters Point Youth Opportunity Center (1965-1966), a planning consultant for the Bay Area Social Planning Council (1966-1967), director of the Concentrated Employment Program of San Francisco Economic Opportunity Council

(1966-1967), and a senior consultant with Social Dynamics (1968-1970), a corporation specializing in manpower programs. A part-time lecturer at San Francisco State College, the University of California, and Berkeley Graduate School of Social Welfare, he was elected to the Berkeley City Council in 1967 and served until 1971. He was elected to the Ninety-second Congress, and has been subsequently reelected up through the current Ninety-Eighth Congress. He is married to the former Leone Roscoe.

•DENVER, JAMES WILLIAM, (1817-1892) - U. S. representative from California, was born in Winchester, Virginia, and attended the public schools. He moved to Ohio in 1830 with his parents, who settled near Wilmington.

He taught school in Missouri in 1841, was graduated from the Cincinnati Law School in 1844; was admitted to the bar and commenced practice in Xenia, Ohio. He also published the *Thomas Jefferson.* He moved to Platte City, Missouri in 1845 and continued the practice of law. He served as captain in the Twelfth Regiment, United States Infantry, during the war with Mexico, and then moved to California in 1850.

Elected to the State senate in 1851, he was appointed secretary of state in 1852, and was elected as an Anti-Broderick Democrat to the Thirty-fourth Congress (March 1, 1855-March 3, 1857). He was not a candidate for renomination in 1856. Appointed Commissioner of Indian Affairs April 17, 1857, he resigned to become Governor of the Territory of Kansas June 17, 1857.

During his administration gold was found on Cherry Creek, and the present capital of Colorado (then Kansas Territory) was found and named "Denvor" for the chief executive. Reappointed Commissioner of Indian Affairs November 8, 1858, he served until his resignation on March 32, 1859. During the Civil War, he was commissioned brigadier general in the Union Army August 14, 1861. After resigning from the Army March 5, 1863, he resumed the practice of his profession in Washington, D.C., and Wilmington, Ohio. He was a delegate to the Democratic National Conventions in 1876, 1880, and 1884. He died in Washington, D.C.

•DEUKMEJIAN, GEORGE "DUKE", (1928-) - thirty-fifth
governor of California (1983-), was born in Menands, New York,
to George and Alice Gairden Deukmejian. He graduated from
nearby Siena College in 1949 with a B.A. degree in sociology and
earned a J.D. from St. John's University law school in 1952.
From 1953 to 1955, Deukmejian fought in the Korean War
with the U.S. Army. Shortly afterwards, he met Gloria Saatjian
and married her in 1957. He began his political career as a deputy
county counsel in Los Angeles while working with a Long Beach
law firm. In 1963, he took a seat in the state assembly, and four
years later he was elected a state senator from his district. As a
legislator, he authored over 180 laws, most of which related to
crime, including the "Use a Gun, Go to Prison" act and the
state's death penalty statute. He acted as senate majority leader
during 1969-71, and minority whip in 1974-78. In 1978, he was
elected Attorney General of California, where he continued his
anti-crime stance. Four years later, he had garnered enough support from conservatives in the state to run for the governorship.
He won after a tight race with Los Angeles mayor Tom Bradley,
and took his seat in the newly-restored state Capitol.

Governor Deukmejian has had to deal with large deficits in
the state budget since taking office. Rather than raise taxes, he
has planned major cuts in state programs such as higher education and medical aid in order to make ends meet. The governor
visited his wife and three children in Long Beach on weekends until the mansion outside of Sacramento was readied for them.

•DICKINSON, ANGIE BROWN, (1932-) - actress, was born
Angeline Brown in Kulm, North Dakota, where her parents
published the local newspaper. She grew up in Kulm and
Edgeley, North Dakota, and Glendale, California.

She attended Catholic schools, Immaculate Heart College,
and studied secretarial science at Glendale College. Also attended Batami Schneider's acting workshop and took singing and
dancing lessons.

She worked as a secretary for an aircraft company, but

began her acting career by entering a local television beauty contest. Her winning led to a place in the chorus line of the network television show, "The Colgate Comedy Hour" starring Jimmy Durante. Continued to work as a secretary while looking for parts in television shows. Made motion picture debut in the 1954 film *Lucky Me*, and had small roles in *Man with the Gun*, *Tennessee's Partner* and *Tension at Table Rock* (1956). Discovered by director-producer Howard Hawks, she signed to a seven year contract. Her first major role was in *Rio Bravo* in 1959, starring John Wayne and Dean Martin, which has been called her best performance. Her contract with Hawks was sold to Warner Brothers, where she was used in a series of supporting roles from 1960 to 1962, when she made her Broadway debut in *The Perfect Set Up*, a comedy starring Gene Barry and Jan Sterling, which closed after five performances. She starred in the film, *Jessica* in 1962 and signed a seven year contract at Universal, and then starred opposite Gregory Peck in *Captain Newman*, for Universal in 1964. She played supporting roles in a series of films for Universal from 1964 to 1965, until she won release from her contract. She continued to appear in films for a number of studios until 1973. She starred in the NBC television series "Police Woman" from 1974 to 978, which became the top-rated show on television in 1975 and for which she received three Emmy Award nominations. She made a comeback in 1980 with her role in *Dressed to Kill*, and starred in NBC television series "Cassie & Co.," in 1982. Other films include *Ocean's 11* (1960), *Point Blank* (1968), and *Pretty Maids All in la Row* (1971).

She was married to Gene Dickinson, whom she divorced in 1959. In 1965, she married Burt Bacharach. She was divorced in 1980.

•DIDION, JOAN, (1934-) - author, was born in Sacramento, California, the daughter of Eugene Jerrett and Frank Reese Didion and graduated from public high school before receiving a B.A. in English literature from the University of California, Berkeley in 1856.

Didion began writing in her early teens, copying pages from the works of Hemingway and Conrad in order to discover their styles. She worked as editor of her college newspaper, and won a job at *Vogue* magazine as a result of an article she wrote on a San Francisco architect. Within a few years, she became associate feature editor and was a regular contributor to *Mademoiselle, National Review,* and the *Saturday Evening Post.* In 1963, she took a leave of absence from *Vogue* to work on her first novel and never took a "regular" job again. She wrote *Run River* when she was homesick for her old life in Sacramento. "That's why there's too much landscape in it, too much social detail," she told *Newsday* later. However, she received favorable reviews that cited her technical abilities and feeling for language.

Didion moved to the Los Angeles area in 1964, with her husband and fellow writer, John Dunne. The two wrote a column for the *Saturday Evening Post* called "Points West" in 1967 to 1969, and Didion continued writing freelance articles for other major publications. Her *Slouching Towards Bethlehem* in 1968 gave her the reputation of a sharp observer "and interpreter of American doubts, feelings and realities..." In it, she mirrored the hippie generation as if she had become part of it, which she had for a time. Her next books were novels, set in the Southwest and Central America. She told the *Chicago Tribune, "An awful lot of stuff in my novels came out of stuff I encountered reporting,"* and she *has continued over the years to report through various columns on the tempo of the times. She also co-authored the screenplays for the films Panic in Needle Park,* 1971, *and A Star is Born,* 1976.

Her most recent book, *The White Album,* is the events of the 1960s as reflected on Ms. Didion's own life. She explores the horrors of the Manson family and the Ferguson brothers, the creation of J. P. Getty's museum in Los Angeles, the women's movement, Black Panthers, and the lifestyle of people usually lumped together as "the hippies." Once again the stories are told in the voice of a southern California.

Although she is fascinated by what goes on in the world Ms. Didion is apolitical and does not get involved in causes of women's liberation concerns. "The politics I want are anarchic. Throw out laws. Tear it down. Start all over." is what she has told a *New York Times Book Review* writer. She continues to write freelance articles and a column with her husband for *California* magazine.

•**DISNEY, WALTER E.**, (1901-66) - amuzement park developer, and a creator of animated films, left his hometown of Chicago for Hollywood in 1923. By 1928, he had achieved phenomenal success with the release of an animated talking film of his cartoon character Mickey Mouse. Throughout the following years, Disney continued to create whimsical cartoon characters and animated stories such as the full-length production of *Snow White*. He became tremendously popular for his humor and technical ability, and in 1940 he opened his own studio with hundreds of employees. After *Snow White*, he developed and supervised the production of both animated films and nature movies showing animals in their natural habitats.

In 1955, he developed a fantasy-amusement land in the then undeveloped area of Anaheim in Orange County. After his death, another one of his plans for a Disneyworld in Orlando, Florida, was built by his massive studio. Films with the Disney trademark are still being produced, and Disneyland celebrated its 25th anniversary in 1979.

•**DIXON, JULIAN CAREY** (1934-) - U.S. representative from California, was born in Washington, D.C., and attended the public schools. After moving to Los Angeles, he graduated from Dorsey High School (1953), Los Angeles State College (B.A. 1962), and Southwestern University (LL.B 1967). He was a sergent in the United States Army. In 1972, he became a member of the California State Assembly, a position he retained until 1978, when he was elected as a Democrat to the Ninety-Sixth Congress. Reelected in 1978 and 1980, he is a member of the current Ninety-Eighth Congress.

•**DOCKWILER, JOHN FRANCIS,**)1895-1943) - U.S. representative from California, was born in Los Angeles, California and attended parochial schools. He graduated from Loyola College in Los Angeles in 1918 and from the University of southern Caliornia in 1921. He attended the law department of Harvard University in

Cambridge, Massachusetts; was admitted to the bar September 6, 1921, and commenced practice in Los Angeles in 1922. Elected as a Democrat to the Seventy-third, Seventy-fourth, and Seventy-fifth Congresses (March 4, 1933-January 3, 1939), he was not a candidate for renomination in the primaries in 1938, but was an unsuccessful candidate for nomination as Governor. In the general election, he was an unsuccessful Independent candidate for reelection to the Seventy-sixth Congress. He resumed the practice of law and was later district attorney of Los Angeles County (1940-1943). He died in Los Angeles.

•DORNAN, ROBERT K. (1933-) - U.S. representative from California, was born in New York City and graduated from Loyola High School in California in 1950. He attended Loyoloa University from 1950 until 1953, when he joined the United States Air Force. He served as a fighter pilot from 1953 to 1958. Later, he was a broadcaster-journalist, a commerical pilot, and an award-winning television producer, winning Emmies in 1968 and 1969 for a daily program he hosted entitled, "Tempo." From 1969 to 1973, he produced and hosted the "Robert K. Dornan Show" for a Los Angeles television station. An active supporter of civil rights, he was also involved in the campaign to bring attention to the plight of the American Prisoners of War and Missing in Action in Vietnam. Elected to the Ninety-fifth Congress in 1976, he was reelected to each succeeding Congress before leaving office at the end of the Ninety-Seventh Congress in January, 1983. He is married to Sallie Hansen.

•DOUGLAS, HELEN GAHAGAN, (1900-1980 - U. S. representative from California was born in Boonton, Morris County, New Jersey, and attended the public schools, Berkeley School for Girls in Brooklyn, New York, Capen School for Girls in Northampton, Massachusetts, and Barnard College at Columbia University, New York city.

She moved to Los Angeles, California in 1931, and engaged in the theatrical profession and also as an opera singer (1922-1938), Democratic National committeewoman for California (1940-1944) and vice chairman of the Democratic state central committee, she was chairman of the women's division (1940-1944). She was a member of the national advisory committee of the Works Progress Administration and of the state committee on the National Youth Administration in 1939 and 1940. A member of the board of governors of the California Housing and Planning Association in 1942 and 1943, she was appointed by President Franklin D. Roosevelt as a member of the Voluntary Participation Committee, Office of Civilian Defense. She was also appointed by President Harry S. Truman as alternate United States Delegate to the United Nations Assembly. Elected as a Democrat to the Seventy-ninth, Eightieth, and Eighty-first Congresses (January 3, 1945-January 3, 1951), she was not a candidate for renomination in 1950, but instead ran unsuccessfully for the United States Senate against Richard M. Nixon. The campaign was a bitter one in which Nixon used the national hysteria over communism against the liberal Douglas.

She returned to the theatre after the defeat, and continued to actively support liberal causes as a private citizen. One of the last times she appeared in the public eye came in 1979 when she spoke to a U.S. congressional hearing, asking that federal funds be given for cancer research. She died of cancer a year later.

•DOWNEY, JOHN G., (1826-1894) - seventh Governor of California (1860-1862), was born in County Roscommon, Ireland. His grandfather, John, of Castle Sampson, and his father, Dennis Downey, were stock farmers.

John G. left home and reached California in 1849 with but $10 in his pocket. He settled in Los Angeles in 1850, and in three years had accumulated $30,000. He then engaged in stock raising and real estate operations. He became quite prosperous and purchased about 75,000 acres of land, near the present sites of Downey, Wilmington, San Pedro, and elsewhere. He was the owner of the Santa Gertrude ranch, noted for its beauty and mineral springs. He was elected governor in 1860, succeeding in office Governor Latham, with whom he had acted as lieutenant-governor in 1859. "His administration as governor was universally commended." says Bancroft, "and as a private citizen, one to whose enterprise and liberalitry is largely due the properity of Southern California, he is no less widely esteemed." It was during this administration that support for the U.S. governmnent in the civil war was established. But many influential business men thought that nothing which California could do would have any effect upon the result of the national controversy, and counseled neutrality. One of the United States senators from California had even said in the Senate: "If ever the Federal Union shall be broken up, the eastern boundary of the Pacific republic will be, in my opinion, the Sierra Madre and the Rocky Mountains." Against this and other utterances the San Francisco *Bulletin* said, "The repudiation of the Pacific republic notion by California, and her decoration against secession in any form, may prove an important step toward restoring the harmony to the country." On April 24, 1801, the news was received at San Francisco that Fort Sumter had surrendered, and that blood had been spilled. Both political parties professed devotion to the national cause. On May 11th, business was suspended in San Francisco as a loyal demonstration. On May 17th, the legislature pledged the state of California to the support of the government.

Downey completed the balance of Latham's term. He was then defeated for election in 1862. He died on March 1, 1894.

•DOWNEY, SHERIDAN, (1884-1961) - U. S. senator from California, was born in Laramie, Wyoming and attended the public schools. He graduated from the law department of the University of Michigan at Ann Arbor in 1907, was admitted to the bar the same year and commenced practice in Laramie. He moved to Sacramento, California in 1913 and continued the practice of law. Elected as a Democrat to the United States Senate in 1938 he was reelected in 1944 and served from January 3, 1939, until his resignation November 30, 1950, due to ill health. He was not a candidate for renomination in 1950. He died in San Francisco.

•DOYLE, CLYDE GILMAN, (1887-1963) - U. S. representative from California, was born in Oakland, California and attended public schools there and in Seattle, Washington, before graduating from the College of Law of the Univerity of Southern California at Los Angeles in 1918.

Admitted to the bar in 1918, he commenced practice in Long Beach. He was a member and president of the Board of Freeholders (1921-1922), the board of trustees of Adelaide Tichenor Hospital-School for Crippled Children, and the California State Board of Education. He received the Meritorious Citizenship Award from the Interallied Council of Service Clubs of Long Beach in 1936. He was elected as a Democrat to the seventy-ninth Congress in 1945. An unsuccessful candidate for relection in 1946 to the Eightieth Congress, he was elected to the Eighty-first and to the seven succeeding Congresses and served from 1949 until his death in Arlington, Virginia.

•DOZER, DONALD MARQUAND, (1905-) - historian and educator, was born in Zanesville, Ohio, to Perley and Minnie Dozer and was educated at College of Wooster (B.A), and Harvard (M.A., Ph.D). In 1959, he was hired as an associate professor of history at the University of California at Santa Barbara. Five years later he was made a full professor. When he retired in 1972, he was given the title of professor emeritus. He has been a member of the American Historical Association, American Society of International Law and the Pacific Coast Council on Latin American Studies. Considered a leading authority on Latin American History, he has published several books on that subject. He is married to Alice Louis Scott.

•DREIER, DAVID T. (1952-) - U.S. representative from California, was born in Kansas City, Missouri, and graduated from Claremont Men's College with a B.A. (cum laude) in political science in 1975. The following year he received an MA. in American Government from Claremont Graduate School. From 1975 to 1979, he was director of corporate relations and assistant director of college relations for the Men's College. A member of the Republican state Central Committee, he was elected as a Republican to the Ninety-seventh Congress on November 4, 1980. Two years later, he was reelected to the current Ninety-eighth Congress.

•DYMALLY, MERVYN M. (1926-) - U.S. representative from California, was born in Cedros, Trinidad, West Indies, and attended the Cedros Government School in Trinidad. He later attended the St. Benedict and Naparima Secondary in San Fernanado, Trinidad, before graduating from California State University (B.A. 1954, M.A. 1969) and the United States International University (Ph.D 1978). President of the Mervyn M Dymally Company, he has also worked as a lecturer and teacher. In 1962, he was elected to the California Assembly. He left the Assembly four years later when he was elected to the state Senate. He served as a state senator from 1966 to 1975 and as the state's Lieutenant Governor from 1975 until 1979. He was elected as a Democrat to the Ninety-seventh Congress on November 4, 1980, and was reelected to the current Ninety-Eighth Congress two years later. He married the former Alice M. Gueno in 1968.

E

•EATON, THOMAS MARION, (1896-1939) - U.S. representative from California, was born on a farm near Edwardsville, Madison County, Illinois, and attended the country schools and Edwardsville High School. He graduated from the State Normal School in Normal, Illinois, in 1917 and served as principal of the Lincoln grade school in Clinton, Illinois, in 1917 and 1918.

During the First World War, Eaton served in the United States Navy as an ensign. He moved to Long Beach, California, in 1921 and engaged in the automobile sales business.

Elected to the city council in 1934, reelected in 1936, he was unanimously chosen mayor by the council. Elected as a Republican to the Seventy-sixth Congress, he served from January 3, 1939, until his death in Long Beach.

•EBENSTEIN, WILLIAM, (1910-1976) - educator, was born in Australia to Samuel and Gittel R. Ebenstein and earned a Ph.D at the University of Wisconsin (1928) and an LL.D from the University of Vienna (1928). He taught at the Wisconsin university for several years before joining the faculty at Princeton in 1946. He became a professor of political science at University of California, Santa Barbara, in 1962 and remained there until his death. Considered an authority on totalitarian government, he authored several books including *Great Political Thinkers, Modern Political Thought, Today's Isms,* and *Two Ways of Life.* He was married to Ruth Barbara Jaburek.

•EDWARDS, DON - U.S. representative from California, was born in San Jose, California, and attended the public schools there. He graduated from Stanford University and Stanford Law School (1936-1938). After being admitted to the state bar, he became a special agent for the Federal Bureau of Investigation (1940-1941), and then served in the United State Navy during World War II as a gunnery officer and in Naval Intelligence. After the war, he became a businessman. Elected to the Eighty-eighth Congress in 1962, he was reelected to each succeeding Congress up to the current Ninety-eighth Congress.

•ELLIOTT, ALFRED JAMES, (1895-1973) - U. S. representative from California, was born in Guinda, Yolo County, California and moved with his parents to Winters, California, in 1901 and to Tulare, California, in 1910. He attended the public schools, and later engaged in farming and livestock raising. He was secretary-manager of the Tulare County Fair for many years, beginning in 1929. Owner and publisher of a newspaper, he was chairman of the board of supervisors of Tulare County (1933-1937) and served on the California State Safety Council in 1936.

A member of the California Supervisor Association of the State welfare board in 1935 and 1936, he was elected as a Democrat to the Seventy-fifth Congress to fill the vacancy caused by the death of Henry E. Stubbs. Reelected to the Seventy-sixth and to the four succeeding Congreses, he served from May 4, 1927, to January 3, 1949, but was not a candidate for renomination in 1948 to the Eighty-first Congress. When his final term ended, he became president of Tulare Daily News. Later, he was a farmer and livestock breeder.

•ELSTON, JOHN ARTHUR, (1874-1921) - U. S. representative from California, was born in Woodland, Yolo County, California and attended the public schools. He graduated from Hesperian College in 1892 and the University of California at Berkeley in 1897. He then engaged in educational work, studied law, was admitted to the bar (1901) and commenced practice in Berkeley.

An executive secretary to the Governor of California (1903-1907) he was a member of the board of trustees of the State Institution for the Deaf and Blind (1911-1914). Elected as a Progressive Republican to the Sixty-fourth and to the three succeeding Congresses, he served from March 4, 1915, until his death in Washington, D.C.

•ELTSE, RALPH ROSCOE, (1885-) - U. S. representative from California, was born in Oskaloosa, Mahaska County, Iowa, and attended the public schools. He graduated from Penn College, Oskaloosa, Iowa, in 1909 and from Haverford College in Pennsylvania in 1910. Moving to Berkeley, California, in 1912, he attended the law department of the University of California, was admitted to the bar in 1915, and commenced practice there.

A member of the Republican State committee (1932-1935) and a delegate to the Republican State conventions in 1932, 1934, and 1940, he was elected as a Republican to the Seventy-third Congress (March 4, 1933-January 3, 1935), but was an unsuccessful candidate for election in 1934 to the Seventy-fourth congress and in 1940 to the Seventy-seventh Congress. When his term ended, he resumed the practice of law.

•ENSMINGER, MARION EUGENE, (1908-) - animal scientist and educator, was born in Stover, Missouri, and was educated at University of Missouri (B.S. 1931, M.S. 1932) and University of Minnesota (Ph.D 1941). Ensminger is president of Consultant-Agriservices of Clovis, California. He has served as the first president of the American Society of Agricultural Consultants and has received the title of Distinguished Professor at Wisconsin State University, River Falls. He was also the recipient of the Distinguished Teacher Award of the American Society of Animal Science. He has written and edited numerous books, and has contributed articles for scientific journals, livestock magazines and trade publications. Since 1973, he has served as an adjunct professor at California State University of Fresno. He is married to Audrey Helen Watts.

•ENTRY.US JOHN B., (1812-1875) - fifth governor of California (1858-1860), was born in Ohio, and was a congressman from that state from 1839 to 1845.

He then served as the lieutenant-colonel of an Ohio regiment in the Mexican war, becoming its commander at the death of its colonel at Monterey. He was appointed by President Taylor a commissioner to settle the Mexican boundary under the treaty of Guadalupe Hidalgo, but on migrating to California about 1850, he resigned his place as boundary commissioner, and devoted himself to law and politics.

He was regarded as a pro-slavery Democrat, and was soon elected United States senator, sitting in the Senate from March 17, 1851 to March 3, 1857. He was United States minister to Mexico from November 7, 1860 to May 14, 1861. It was during Weller's administration that the long-standing differences between United States senators Gwin and David C. Broderick, both of California, and both leaders of opposing wings of the Democratic party in that state, came to a head. They were ended in a duel between Broderick and David S. Terry, for four years judge of the state supreme court, who resigned his office and challenged Broderick.

The first meeting of the parties was in San Mateo county, ten miles from San Francisco, but was interrupted by the officers of the law. The next morning (September 13, 1859) they met again and proceeded to the first act. When the word was given Broderick's pistol was discharged before it reached a level. The ball struck the earth in a direct line with, but at some distance from, his antogonist, who stood cool and firm. Broderick sank to the ground, mortally wounded. He died on September 16. To those around his deathbed he remarked, "They killed me because I was opposed to the extension of slavery and to a corrupt administration."

•EU, MARCH FONG, (1927-) - California secretary of state, was born in Oakdale, California, the daughter of Yuen Kong and Shiu Shee Kong. After attending high school in Richmond, California and Salinas Junior College, she received a B.S. from the University of California, Berkeley, in 1948, an M.E. from Mills College in 1951, and an Ed.D. from Stanford University in 1956. She also undertook post-graduate study at Columbia University, New York, and California State University, Hayward, California, and obtained California teaching credentials in secondary and junior college health and development. Her first job was a dental hygienist in the Oakland public schools from 1945 to 1948, when she became chairman of the division of dental hygiene at the University of California Medical Center, San Francisco. At the same time, she was supervisor of dental health education for the Alameda county schools and served as lecturer in health education at Mills College (1957-58).

Elected to the Alameda County Board of Education in 1956 and named president in 1961, she served as president of the Alameda County School Boards Association in 1965 and worked as Educational and Legislative Consultant for a number of groups from 1962 to 1966, including the Bureau of Intergroup Relations, California State Department of Education, and several school districts.

First elected to office in the state of California when she became the Assemblywoman for Oakland and Castro Valley in 1966, she was reelected in 1968, 1970 and 1972 by increasing majorities. Elected secretary of the state of California in 1974 with over 3.4 million votes--the highest number of votes received by any of the constitutional officers in that general election--she was the first woman elected to that office in the history of California, as well as the first woman of Asian ancestry elected to statewide office. Reelected in 1978 and 1982, she was also named the California Chief of Protocol in 1975. She is married to Henry Eu.

•EVANS, WILLIAM ELMER, (1877-1959_ - U. S. representative from California, was born near London, Laurel County, Kentucky, and attended the public schools and Sue Bennett Memorial College. He studied law, was admitted to the bar in 1902 and commenced practice in London before moving to Glendale, California in 1910. He engaged in the practice of law and in banking, in Glendale, where he became city attorney (1911-1921). A delegate to the Republican National Convention at Cleveland in 1924, he was elected as a Republican to the Seventieth and to the three succeeding Congresses (March 4, 1927-January 3, 1935). An unsuccessful candidate for reelection in 1934 to the Seventy-fourth Congress, he was involved in the practice of law, real-estate development, and ranching until his death in Los Angeles.

F

•FAGES, PEDRO, (1730-94) - Spanish governor of Northern California, was a native Catalonian who left for Mexico as an infantry lieutenant in 1767; two years later he was made military head of the sailing division of the Sacred Expedition from Baja to Alta California under the leadership of Portola. He was with the group of Portola and his men when they discovered the San Francisco Bay, and when the leader left to return to Mexico, Fages was named governor of that area in 1770. At that time, however, Spanish occupation of Alta California was held at two points 450 miles apart, with Fages to the north and Father Juniperio Serra and his missions to the south. Fages repeatedly refused to grant Serra permission to build more missions, claiming he didn't have the soldiers to defend them, and their differences deepened into a feud. While Fages led expeditions through the Salinas and Santa Clara valleys, which at times provided food for the early California settlements, Fr. Serra traveled to Mexico City to complain of Fages' refusals for missions.

In 1774 the governor was ordered to new assignments, including service in wars against the Apaches, but he returned eight years later as governor of Alta California. Although the old feud with Fr. Serra resumed with his return, the governor's new wife, Dona Eulalia, brought about the liveliest disputes. Her dissatisfaction with the crude, isolated life in Monterey led her to push for a divorce from Fages, basing her complaint on an alleged affair with an Indian girl. This scandalized the early settlement padres, but eventually lthe lively young woman reconciled with her husband. However, she pushed for Fages' retirement until he finally conceded in 1791 to spend his last years in Mexico. He wrote, *A Historical, Political and Natural Description of California* in 1775.

•**FAZIO, VIC** (1942-) - U.S. representative from California, was born in Winchester, Massachusetts, and attended the public schools of New Jersey. He graduated from Union College in Schenectady, New York, (B.A. 1965) and then did graduate work in public administration at the California State University in Sacramento. He was a congressional and legislative consultant from 1966 until 1975, when he became a member of the California Assembly. He was a member of the Sacramento County Charter Commission and the county planning commission. He was also the cofounder of the California Journal Magazine. On November 7, 1978, he was elected as a Democrat to the Ninety-sixth Congress. Reelected twice, he is a member of the current Ninety-eighth Congress.

•**FEINSTEIN, DIANNE GOLDMAN,** (1933-) - Mayor of San Francisco, was born in San Francisco to Betty Rosenburg, a model, and Leon Goldman, a physician, and attended Convent of the Sacred Heart High School in San Francisco. She received a B.S. in history and political science from Stanford University in 1955.

As a public affairs intern with the Coro Foundation, Feinstein discovered her interest in California government. She was an administrative assistant with the California Industrial Welfare Commission in 1956 to 1957, where she gained her first professional experience. When her daughter was born, she stayed at home for five years, and then took a job as a member of the California Women's Board of Terms and Paroles, where she set the terms of paroles for women convicts in the state. She was subsequently appointed to the city and county Advisory Commission for Adult Detention in San Francisco in 1966, and to the Mayor's Commission on Crime the next year. In 1969, she had been successful enough to win a seat on the city's board of supervisors. By 1970, she was elected president of the board, a position she held until 1972, and again in 1974 to 1976. In the meantime, she tried to be elected mayor in 1971 against the favored Democratic Mayor Joseph Alioto, but lost. Feinstein continued to be identified with the liberal faction in San Francisco politics, however, and gained the nickname of "Mrs. Clean" when she tried to ban pornography and violent depictions of sex in the North Beach nightclub section of the city. She lost again in the 1975 mayoral election, but continued her work on the board of supervisors. In 1978, Mayor George Moscone and a fellow supervisor, Harvey Milk were shot and killed at city hall, and Feinstein was elected by the other members of the board to fill the rest of the mayor's term. She defeated Supervisor Quentin Kopp in the next election despite the fact that Kopp had received Governor Jerry Brown's endorsement, but Feinstein managed to appeal to the various groups that make up the political force of San Francisco, including the large homosexual community.

She was married to Jack Berman, a lawyer in the 1950s. Divorced in 1962, she remarried Bertram Feinstein, a neurosurgeon, in 1962. After he died in 1978, she remarried banker Richard Blum in January, 1980.

•FELTON, CHARLES NORTON, (1828-1914) - U. S. representative and senator from California was born in Buffalo, New York and attended Syracuse Academy. He studied law, was admitted to the bar but never practiced and went to California in 1849. He engaged in mercantile pursuits there and afterward in banking. He was sheriff of Yuba County in 1853 and subsequently tax collector. Appointed treasurer of the United States Mint at San Francisco and Assistant Treasurer of the United States, he served from September 4, 1868 to April 23, 1877. A member of the State assembly (1878-1882) he was elected as a Republican to the Forty-ninth and Fiftieth Congresses (March 4, 1885-March 3, 1889), but was not a candidate for renomination. Elected to the United States Senate to fill the vacancy caused by the death of George Hearst, he served from March 19, 1891 to March 3, 1893, but was not a candidate for reelection. Later, he was state prison director (1903-1907) and a presidential elector on the Republican ticket of Taft and Butler (1912). He died at his home in Menlo Park, California.

•FICKERT, CHARLES MARRON (1873-1937) - lawyer, was born in Bear Valley, California, to Frederick William and Mary Glynn Fickert. His father, a rancher, came from Prussia to San Francisco in 1850. Charles Fickert graduated from Stanford University in 1898. He was captain of the Stanford football team in 1896 and coach in 1902. Admitted to the California bar in 1899, he began practicing in San Francisco in the office of Edward Robson Taylor. From 1903 to 1905,he was assistant U.S. district attorney and in 1909 was elected district attorney of San Francisco. He served in that office until 1920 when he was defeated for reelection. As district attorney for San Franciswco, Fickert became a national figure as prosecutor of Thomas J. Mooney and Warren K. Billings for alleged complicity in the "preparedness" parade bomb explosion of July 22, 1916, whyich killed six persons and seriously injured at least twenty-five others. The only clue to the perpetrators of the act was an anonymous communication sent to the newspapers the day before threatening "a little direct action" to demonstrate that "militarism cannot be forced upon us and our children without a violent protest." Fickert secured the convection with death sentences of both Billings and Mooney in 1917. Almost immediately charges were made by labor organizations that the convection had been obtained by perjured testimony, and a new trial was recommened by John B. Densmore, investigator and solicitor of the U.S. Department of Labor. However, in a special election under California's law for the recall of public officers, held in 1917, Fickert was retained and in 1919, he was exonerated by a grand jury. During this period, several attempts were made on his life, bombs were sent to hime through the mails, and his home was under police guard. He was defeated in a race for the governorship in 1918 and in a second race for district attorney in 1923. Fickert resumed the private practice of law in 1923, in Los Angeles with Gordon M. Gale, continuing until 1931, when the governor appointed him attorney for the California board of medical examiners in Sacramento. He held his position until 1933 when he resigned to return to practicing law in San Francisco. He married Ethel Wallace in 1905. He died in San Francisco.

•FIEDLER, BOBBI (1937-) - U.S. representative from California, was born in Santa Monica, California, and graduated from Santa Monica High School in 1979. She attended Santa Monica City College and Santa Monica Technical School. She later owned and operated two pharmacies. One of the cofounders of the antibusing organization BUSSTOP, she was elected Los Angeles City Board of Education in 1977. A Republican, she was elected to the Ninety-Seventh Congress in 1980, and was reelected two years later.

•**FILIPPI, FRANK JOSEPH,** (1907-) - attorney, was born in San Francisco, California, and received a B.A. degree from Lincoln University (1928) and an LL.B from University of San Francisco (1932). Filippi is senior partner of the Mullen & Filippi law firm of San Francisco. Previously he was senior counsel and also statewide claims superintendent for the Insurance Fund of California. He served with the American Red Cross from 1942 to 1946. He is recognized as an authority on the laws of Workmen's Compensation and related fields. He is past president and director of the Lawyer's Club of San Francisco and a member of the American Bar Association, Inter-American Bar Association and the San Francisco Bar Association. He is married to Olivia Cotta.

•**FITZGERALD, FRANCES SCOTT KEY,** (1896-1940) - author, wrote under the name F. Scott Fitzgerald, was born in St. Paul, Minnesota, to Edward and Mary McQuillan Fitzgerald. Through his maternal great-grandparents, he was related to Francis Scott Key, author of the "The Star Spangled Banner." Fitzgerald was educated at the Newman school in Hackensack, New Jersey, and at Princeton University. In his senior year (1917) he left Princeton to join the U.S. army in World War One, serving as second lieutenant in the 45th infantry and first lieutenant in the 67th infantry, and as aide-de-camp to Brig. Gen. James A. Ryan. Upon his discharge in 1919, he began writing professionally. His early work, which pictured American youth in its postwar restlessness and rejection of restraining traditions, was published in the *Saturday Evening Post* and numerous other leading publications of the day. He developed this new vein of fiction in two novels, *This Side of Paradise* (1920) and *The Beautiful and* *the Damned* (1922), and in two collections of short stories, *Flappers and Philosophers* (1920) and *Tales of the Jazz Age*. During the 1920s, he lived among the expatriate artists who were gathered in Paris. He wrote *The Vegetable,* a play, in 1923, and *The Great Gatsby,* a novel, in 1925, and *All the Sad Young Men,* a volume of short stories, in 1926. In 1934, his novel, *Tender is the Night,* ran in four installments in *Scribner's Magazine* before its publication as a book. In the late 1930s, Fitzgerald moved to Hollywood to work on screen plays for Metro-Goldwyn-Mayer studios. He died in Hollywood while working on his final novel, *The Last Tycoon.* He marrried Zelda Sayre in 1920.

•**FLETCHER, CHARLES KIMBALL,** (1902-) - U. S. representative from California, born in San Diego, California and attended the public schools. He graduated from Stanford University of California in 1924, and also attended Pembroke College, Oxford University, England in 1934. He then worked in the savings and loan business. During World War II, he served as a lieutenant with the United States Naval Reserve from 1943 to 1945. Elected as a Republican to the Eightieth Congress (January 3, 1947-January 3, 1949), he was an unsuccessful candidate for reelection in 1948 to the Eighty-first Congress. President and manager of the Home Federal Savings & Loan Association (1934-1959) and chairman of its board of directors since 1959, he was a member of California Commission on Correctional Facilities and Services (1955-1957).

•**FLINT, FRANK PUTMAN,** (1861-1929) - U. S. senator from California was born in North Reading, Middlesex County, Massachusetts, and moved in 1969 with his parents to San Francisco, California where he attended public schools. He moved to Los Angeles in 1887 and served as deputy United States marshall (1888-1892). He was appointed clerk in the district attorney's office in 1892. Meanwhile, he studied law, was admitted to the bar on October 10, 1892, and commenced practice in Los Angeles. An assistant United States attorney in 1892 and 1893 he was judge of the superior court of Los Angeles County from 1895 until 1897, when he became United States district attorney for the southern district of California, a post he held until 1901. Elected a Republican to the United States Senate, he served from March 4, 1905, to March 3, 1911, but was not a candidate for reelection. He resumed the practice of law in Los Angeles, and engaged in banking. Appointed a member of the state land settlement board in 1917, he was reappointed in 1926 and later served as president of the National Boulder Dam Association and as a trustee of Occidental College. He died in the Philippines while on a world tour.

•FONDA, JANE SEYMOUR, (1937-) - actress and activist, was born in New York City, New York, the daughter of Henry Fonda and Frances Seymour Brokaw Fonda. Her father was a well-known actor, while her brother Peter is also established in the entertainment industry. She was a student at the Greenwich Academy, Greenwich, Connecticut, the Emma Willard School, Troy, New York, and Vassar College for two years. She studied painting in Paris, and later, piano in New York, and then began to study acting at the Actors Studio in 1958. Jane Fonda almost decided not to become an actress. Overwhelmed by the significance of her family name, she was afraid to fail. However, she had no need to be concerned; she was lauded as being the most gifted and the loveliest of the young actesses rising in the late 50s and early 60s, and is referred to as being a natural born comedienne. Her father neither encouraged nor discouraged her, however, when she played opposite him when she was 17, in *The Country Girl* he recognized her inherent talent. In the late 1960s she became an outspoken critic of the Vietnam War and launched herself into a number of social causes.

She was the recipient of the Golden Globe Award, 1978; Golden Apple prize, Female Star of the year, Hollywood Women's Press Club, 1977; Film Critics Award, 1969 and 1971; she received the Academy Award nomination for *They Shoot Horses Don't They* ? 1969; the Academy Award, Best Actress for *Klute*, 1971; and the Academy Award, Best Actress for *Coming Home*, 1978. Other movies she has starred in include *Walk on the Wild Side, Cat Ballou, Barefoot in the Park, Julia, The China Syndrome*, and *Nine to Five*.

She married Roger Vadim in 1966. When that marriage ended in divorce, she married Tom Hayden in 1973. Hayden is a state assemblyman from Los Angeles.

•FORREST, EARLE ROBERT, (1883-) - retired newspaper reporter and author, was born in Washington, Pennsylvania, to Joshua Rhodes and Mary Belle Boyle Forrest and received a B.S. from Washington and Jefferson College. He also studied forestry at the University of Michigan. He is the author of *Missions and Pueblos of the Old Southwest* (1929), *The House of Romance* (1965), *Riding for the Old C.O. Bar* (1964), *The Fabulous Sierra Bonita* (1965), *California Joe,* and other books. He has contributed articles to the *Westerner's Annual Brand Books.* In addition, he has taken hundreds of photographs of Indians in the United States and Mexico since 1902. He is considered one of the first photographer to take a camera among the Navajos in northwestern New Mexico. He was married to Margaret Bingham, who is now deceased, and he resides in his town of birth and San Marino, California.

•FREDERICKS, JOHN DONNAN, (1869-1945) - U. S. representative from California, was born in Burgettstown, Washington County, Pennsylvania and attended the public schools and Washington and Jefferson College. He studied law, was admitted to the bar in 1896 and commenced practice in Los Angeles, California.

He served as an adjutant in the Seventh Regiment, California Volunteer Infantry, during the Spanish-American War in 1898, and was district attorney of Los Angeles County from 1903 to 1915, when he ran unsuccessfully as the Republican candidate for Governor of California. Elected as a Republican to the Sixty-eighth Congress to fill the vacancy caused by the death of Henry Z. Osborne, he was reelected to the Sixty-ninth Congress and served from May 1, 1923, to March 3, 1927. He was not a candidate for renomination in 1926.

After leaving office, he resumed the practice of law at Los Angeles where he died several years later.

•**FREE, ARTHUR MONROE,** (1879-1953) - U.S. representative from California, was born in San Jose, California and attended the public high schools of Santa Clara and the University of the Pacific in Stockton. He graduated from the academic department of Leland Stanford Junior University in Palo Alto in 1901 and from its law department in 1903. Admitted to the bar in 1903, he commenced practice in San Jose, and then moved to Mountain View, where he was city attorney (1904-1910). District attorney of Santa Clara County (1907-1910, he voluntarily retired and resumed the practice of law at San Jose. A delegate to the Republican State conventions in 1914 and from 1920 to 1936, he was elected as a Republican to the Sixty-seventh and to the five succeeding Congresses (March 4, 1921-March 3, 1933). An unsuccessful candidate for reelection in 1932 to the Seventy-third Congress, he resumed the practice of law in San Jose, where he died in 1953.

•**FREDERICKS, JOHN DONNAN,** (1869-1945) - U. S. representative from California, was born in Burgettstown, Washington County, Pennsylvania and attended the public schools and Washington and Jefferson College. He studied law, was admitted to the bar in 1896 and commenced practice in Los Angeles, California.

He served as an adjutant in the Seventh Regiment, California Volunteer Infantry, during the Spanish-American War in 1898, and was district attorney of Los Angeles County from 1903 to 1915, when he ran unsuccessfully as the Republican candidate for Governor of California. Elected as a Republican to the Sixty-eighth Congress to fill the vacancy caused by the death of Henry Z. Osborne, he was reelected to the Sixty-ninth Congress and served from May 1, 1923, to March 3, 1927. He was not a candidate for renomination in 1926.

After leaving office, he resumed the practice of law at Los Angeles where he died several years later.

•**FREMONT, JOHN CHARLES,** (1813-1890) - explorer and military governor of California, led a series of western exploring and scientific expeditions authorized by Congress along the

Oregon trail into the Rockies and California, which established him as a national hero. Born an illegitimate child, Fremont felt the need to establish himself a place in the world. Since he was bright, influential men helped him gain an education, and one of them, Senator Thomas Hart Benton prompted him to lead the expeditions in the hopes of extending American territory. Benton's daughter Jessie soon married Fremont, and her writings of his adventures did much to increase his popularity and favor with the government.

After the first trips to Oregon and California with a party of 40 men (including Kit Carson and Charles Preuss), Fremont again traveled to the Mexican-held territories, but this time he was prepared for military rather than scientific activities. Although he had no official United States authorization, some in Washington, D.C. encouraged Fremont to recruit men with the intent of invading the territory. After laying camp outside of Monterey, Fremont's party was ordered out of California, but the Americans entrenched themselves on Hawk's Peak (now Fremont's Peak) and planted the U.S. flag. Thomas O. Larkin, American consul in Monterey, mediated between Castro and Fremont, and the 60 Americans retreated to the Sacramento Valley. Proceeding northward, Fremont was overtaken at Klamath Lake (Oregon) a few months later by Lt. Archibald H. Gillespie of the Marine Corps, who had come to California disguised as a merchant under the direction of Polk and Buchanan to bring about a peaceful agreement between the *Californios* and the United States. But Gillespie was a high-spirited man like Fremont, and, believing that war with Mexico was imminent, he brought encouraging words from Sen. Benton, and the advice that a bold military action was called for. Fremont then went to Sutter's fort, and led the American settlers in the area to the Bear Flag Revolt. This uprising of about 30 armed settlers led to the capture of the city of Sonoma in June of 1846. This action was quickly overshadowed, however, by the actual outbreak of the Mexican War. Fremont was then commissioned to lead a battalion farther south to suppress revolts and evade ambush. Later, he accepted the surrender of Andres Pico at Cahuenga.

Commodore Robert F. Stockton named Fremont California's military governor, and at the same time, the U.S. government named Kearny as the territory's leader. When Fremont refused to obey Gen. Kearny, he was charged with mutiny, and was courtmartialed in Washington. He was found guilty, but President Polk pardoned him. However, Fremont bitterly refused this clemency and resigned his commission in the army. He was later one of the first two United States Senators elected in California.

In the following years, Fremont wrote accounts of his first expeditions to California in a *Geographical Memoir Upon Upper California* (1848), and then began other expeditions to find a railroad route and gold. He was a millionaire temporarily because of his profits on a mine in Mariposa, and later became the first Republican to run for President (1856), on an anti-slavery platform. During the Civil War, Lincoln appointed him major general in St. Louis and the battlefields of Virginia, where Stonewall Jackson defeated him. His last years were spent as territorial governor of Arizona, and as a promoter of western railroad projects.

G

•**GABLE, CLARK,** (1901-1960) - actor, was born William Clark Gable in Cadiz, Ohio, to William H. Gable and Adeline Hershelman Gable. He was the only child of an oil contractor. When he was seven months old, his mother died. For five years he was raised by his grandparents before his father remarried. Graduating from high school in Hopedale, Ohio, he attended Akron University briefly studying to become a doctor and working at the factory during vacations. Making the acquaintance of some Akron actors, he became interested in the theatre. Spending what free time he had at the theater of an Akron stock company, he began taking minor parts with them. Losing his interest in a medical career, he moved to New York when he was 18 hoping to become an actor. He joined his father in Oklahoma to work in the oil fields, however, when soon, that proved unsuccessful. After saving his money, he was able to quit the oil field job he hated and return to acting. He worked for a small touring company for two years, but was left penniless when the company folded in 1922. Hopping a freight train to Portland, Oregon, he worked in several different jobs before he returned to the theatre.

In 1924, he married Josephine Dillon, the director of a small Portland theatre group he had joined. Soon afterwards, the two moved to Los Angeles seeking work. After several months of little success, Gable was about to leave for Broadway when he finally was given a few small parts. After an unsuccessful screen test, he moved to Texas and then to Broadway. With the backing of Lionel Barrymore, he was given another screen test. Although he failed the test, Gable was given a role in the 1931 movie "The Painted Desert." A few months later, he signed a contract with MGM. For the next twenty-three years he remained in Hollywood with MGM and became one of its largest money-makers of all time. Within a year after signing the contract, Gable was a star. Typecast in tough, sexual roles, Gable won an Oscar in 1934 as best actor in "It Happened One Night." Another Gable film with MGM, "Gone With the Wind," became one of the biggest money-making movies of all times.

When Gable's third wife Carole Lombard was killed in a plane crash in 1939, Gable announced his retirement from acting and enlisted in the United States Army Air Force. He did return to films after the war but his former stardom had faded. Moving to Fox, he made one last great movie, "The Tall Men," but for the most part he became trapped in typecast roles.

During the war, he received the Distinguished Flying Cross and the Air Medal for his valor.

•GAGE, HENRY TIFFT, (1853-1924) - twentieth governor of California (1899-1903), was born near Geneva, New York to D. C. and Catherine (Glover) Gage. During his infancy, his parents moved to East Saginaw, Michigan, where his father entered the practice of law and became judge of the State Circuit Court. He was educated in private schools in Michigan and after spending several years in California, he commenced the study of law in his father's office. He was admitted to the bar in 1873, practiced for two years in Michigan and then located in Los Angeles where he rapidly established a reputation as a careful and well-grounded attorney.

He was married in 1880 to Fanny Rains, the daughter of a pioneer family of Southern California.

In 1888 he was a delegate-at-large to the Republican National Convention, where he made the speech seconding the nomination of Levi P. Morton for the vice-presidency. President Harrison appointed him in 1891 to conduct the prosecution of the Itata crew, but he declined on account of his conviction of the government's error in the matter. In 1898 he was nominated on the Republican ticket for governor of California and he was elected by a large majority. During his administration the office of state veterinarian was created and a law was enacted making it a misdemeanor to desecrate the United States flag by printing on it.

In 1901 Gage became the first California governor to mediate a labor strike. He was unsuccessful in obtaining renomination at the 1902 Republican convention.

In 1909 he was appointed minister to Portugal by President Taft. He resigned in 1911 because of his wife's ill health. Gage died in Los Angeles August 18, 1924.

•GARLAND, HAMLIN, (1860-) - author, was born in West Salem, Massachusetts, to Richard Hayes and Isabel McClintock Garland. His father was an early Wisconsin farmer. In 1869, the family moved to a farm near Osage, Iowa, on which young Hamlin wored as a farm hand for several years. From 1876 to 1881, he attended the Cedar Valley seminary at Osage. When his family moved to Ordway, South Dakota, in 1881, Garland began travelling around the eastern states. Rejoining his family in Dakota in 1883, he took a homestead colain in McPherson county, but a year later sold his claim and went to Boston, where he attended university lectures, read in the public library and taught private classes in English and American literature for three years. He began his career as an author in 1885 by writing several sketches of growing up on an Iowa farm. His impressions as to the loneliness, hardships and drudgery of westyern farm life were presented in a series of stories written in 1887-88, which later were published as *Main Travelled Roads.* In the early 1890s, he changed his literary headquarters from Boston to Chicago, and for several years thereafter, he spent a partr of each summer in the Rocky mountain region of Montana, Colorado and Wyoming to gather backgrounds, settings and characterizations for his stories. in this region he gathered a wealth of fictional and poetic material. In 1895, he made a tour of the Southwest, visiting the ute, Navajo, and Apache Indian reservations. He saw the snake dance at Walpi and wrote one of the earliest popular accounts of that picturesque performance. In 1897, he visited the Sioux and Cheyenne reservations during an uprising, obtaining material for his successful novel, *The Captain of the Gray Horse Troop* (1902). In the spring of 1898, he joined the gold rush to the Kondike, leading a pack-train over the telegraphy trail almost 1000 miles long. Out of that rigorous experience came *The Long Trail* (1907) and many poems. Among his other works are, *A Daughter of the Middle Border,* an autobiographical narrative which won the Pulitzer prize for best biography in 1921, *A Little Norsk* (1891), *Ulysses Grant, His Life and Character* (1898), *The Tyranny of the Dark* (1905), *They of the High Trails* (1912), and *Roadside Meetings* (1930). While in Chicago, he originated and was the first president of the Cliff Dwellers, one of the leading artistic and literary clubs of the west. He was one of the organizers of the National Institute of Arts and Letters and was a director of the American Academy of Arts and Letters. He has received the Litt.D degree from the University of Wisconsin (1926), Beloit College (1931), Northwestern University (1933), and the University of Southern California (1935). He married Zulime Taft in 1899.

•GARLAND, JUDY, (1922-60) - actress, became a Hollywood star as a young girl after performances as a child in vaudeville. Born in Minnesota, she grew up in a film studio where she not only sang, danced, and acted, but went to school. Garland captured the hearts of American moviegoers in the classic *The Wizard of Oz* in 1939, in which she displayed exceptional enthusiasm and a beautifully clear voice. After a number of musical comedies and premature retirement, she returned to films, playing more mature characters such as her roles in *A Star Is Born* and *I Could Go on Singing.*

•GEYER, LEE EDWARD, (1888-1941) - U. S. representative from California was born in Wetmore, Nemaha County, Kansas and attended the public schools. He graduated from Wetmore High School in 1908 and from Baker University in Baldwin City, Kansas in 1922. Afterwards, he did post-graduate work at the University of Wisconsin at Madison and the University of Southern California at Los Angeles. He was a teacher in the rural schools in Nemaha County (1908-1912) and principal of Hamlin High School (1916-1918).

During the First World War, he served as a private in the Third Company, First Battalion, Central Officers' Training School, Camp Grant, Illiniois.
He was principal of Corning High School (1919-1923) in Kansas and Duncan High School (1923-1925) in Arizona. Moving to Los Angeles, California, he was football coach of David Starr Jordan High School (1925-1927) and Bell High School (1927-1929). A teacher of social sciences in Gardena High School (1929-1938), he was a member of the state house of representatives (1934-1936) and an unsuccessful candidate for election in 1936 to the Seventy-fifth Congress. Elected as a Democrat to the Seventy-sixth and Seventy-seventh Congress, he served from January 3, 1939, until his death. He was also a delegate to the Democratic National Convention at Chicago in 1940. He died in Washington, D.C.

•GIANNINI, AMADEO PETER, (1870-1949) - banker, started his tremendously successful career at 12 when he was the clerk of his family's produce firm. Born in San Jose of Italian immigrant parents, Giannini continued to sponsor the Italian community when in 1904 he became director of a savings and loan society catering to them in a neighborhood in San Francisco. The bank was so profitable, he opened a branch in San Jose, and soon had others in both the northern part of the state and the Los Angeles area, despite opposition from other bankers and the Federal Reserve Board. By 1918, he held 24 branches and his bank held the state's fourth largest assets. As the Bank of Italy, it assisted people of little means in obtaining loans, and in 1919, Giannini organized the Bancitaly Corporation to enable him to continue his expansion into branches.
In 1928, he included Bancitaly in a new corporation, Transamerica, assuming control of the Bank of Italy stock and becoming the largest holding company in the world. Two years later, he consolidated even more holdings into the Bank of American National Trust and Savings Association. After the Depression, the retired Giannini became frustrated with his successor's handling of the Transamerica Corporation and by means of proxy fight he ousted the new management and at 62 took over the corporation again. During this time, he served as a University of California

Regent, donating a building and a foundation for agricultural economics at UC Berkeley. Both his son and grandson also served on the UC board.

By 1975, the Bank held assets of $60.4 billion and employed over 60,000 people in 90 countries. Its place as a superpower with holdings, questionable to some, made Bank of America the target of demonstrators and students who attacked its offices, as exemplified when students at the University of California campuses of Santa Barbara and Irvine, where bank branches were burned in 1970. While Giannini's son was president of the corporation, the federal government attacked it for violating the Clayton Anti-Trust Act, which caused the Transamerica Corporation to sever its corporate relations with the Bank.

Today, the non-banking Transamerica Corporation is headquartered in the landmark pyramid-shaped building in San Francisco, on the site of the old Montgomery Block.

•**GIBSON, WELDON BAILEY,** (1917-) - researcher, was born in Eldorado, Texas, to Oscar and Susie Baily Gibson and graduated from Washington State College (B.A. 1938) and Stanford University (M.B.A. 1940, Ph.D 1950). He served in the U.S. Air Force as Colonel from 1941 to 1946. In the latter year, he was named as dean of the Air Force Institute of Technology, a position he held until 1957, when he was hired by Stanford Research Institute as Director of Economics Research and Chairman of International Research. In 1960, he was named executive vice president of the reseach institute, and in 1977, he was named executive vice president of SRI International. Since 1979, he has also served as chairman of the Washington State University Foundation. He is the author or co-author of *Global Geography* (1941), *Pacific Skyways* (1947), and *World Political Geography* (1951). He is married to Helen Mears.

•**GILBERT, EDWARD,** (1819-1852) - U. S. representative, was born in Cherry Valley, Otsego County, New York and attended the public schools. He was a compositor on the *Albany Argus* in 1839 and later an asociate editor.

During the war with Mexico, he served as first lieutenant of Company H in Col. J. D. Stevenson's New York Volunteer Regiment. He arrived with his company in San Francisco in March 1847. He was in command of the detachment and deputy collector of the port of San Francisco in 1847 and 1848, when the regiment was disbanded.

He became founder and editor of the *Alta California* in 1849. Upon the admission of California as a State into the Union, he was elected as a Democrat to the Thirty-first Congress and served from September 11, 1850 to March 3, 1851. He was not a candidate for renomination in 1850.

He was killed in a duel with Gen. James W. Denver, near Sacramento, California.

•GILLETT, JAMES NORRIS, (1860-1937) - twenty-second Governor of California (1907-1911), was born in Viroqua, Wisconsin, to Cyrus Foss and Sarah Jane (Norris) Gillett. His first wife Adelaide Pratt whom he married in 1886 died in 1896. He married Elizabeth Erzgraber in 1898.

Gillett attended public schools in Sparta, Wisconsin, studied law and passed the bar in Wisconsin in 1881. He moved to Eureka, California in 1884 and established a law practice. He served in the state Senate for two terms (1897-1900) and in the state House of Representatives for two terms. The Southern Pacific Railroads political maneuvering won the 1906 Republican gubernatorial nomination for Gillett and he won the election narrowly on a split between the Democrats, Independence League, and Socialist party.

Passage of a direct primary election amendment to the Constitution helped reform the political patronage problems that had long plagued the state.

During the Gillett administration horse racing came under state control and new state buildings were built to replace many destroyed in the earthquake and fire of 1906.

In 1910 Gillett returned to law practice in San Francisco. He died in Berkeley on April 21, 1937.

•**GOERKE, LENOR STEPHEN,** (1912-1972) - educator, was born in Hitchcock, Oklahoma, to Leonard and Nellie Goerke and received a B.S. degree in 1931 from Southeastern State Teachers College, a B.S. and M.D from the University of Oklahoma in 1936, and an M.S. in Public Health Care from University of California, Berkeley, in 1938. After a variety of public health jobs, he was named an associate professor of clinical medicine at University of Southern California in 1951. From 1954 until his death, Goerke was chairman of the Department of Preventive Medicine and Public Health at the School of Medicine, University of California, Los Angeles. At the same time, he was dean of the university's School of Public Health. He was also president of the Los Angeles City Board of Health Commissioners (1961-62), vice president of the California State Board of Health (1962-64), chairman of the Southern California State Advisory Committee to Selective Service, president of the Board of Regents of the American College of Preventive Medicine (1957), president of the Western Branch of the American Public Health Association (1955), and president of the Southern California Public Health Association (1955). He served as a Colonel, M.C., in the United State Army Reserves. He was married to Evelyn Maria Foster in 1938.

•**GOLDWATER, BARRY MORRIS, JR.,** (1928-) - U. S. representative from California, was born in Los Angeles, California and attended grammar school in Phoenix, Arizona, and Staunton Military Academy in Virginia. His father is Barry Morris Goldwater, an Arizona senator and the 1964 Republican candidate for United States president.

The younger Goldwater majored in business and marketing at the University of Colorado and Arizona State University and graduated in 1962. A stockbroker, he was former partner in the firm of Noble Cooke, division of Gregory & Sons, stock brokers. He was elected as a Republican to the Ninety-first Congress by special election, to fill the vacancy caused by the resignation of Ed Reinecke. He was reelected in a general election two years later and served through 1982, when he ran unsuccessfully for the United States Senate.

•GREY, ZANE, (1872-1939), novelist, was born in Zanesville, Ohio to Lewis Grey and Alice Josephine Zane Grey. His father was a jack-of-all-trades. Talented as a baseball player, Grey was actively recruited by several universities; selecting the University of Pennsylvania to study dentistry, he moved to New York shortly after graduating to begin practicing. He quickly tired of the medical profession, however, and decided to devote his life to writing. In 1904, he wrote *Betty Zane*, a historical novel.

Rejected by several publishing companies, Grey packed up his bags and traveled west, eventually settling in California. His experiences in the west inspired Zane to write a new novel. After a few rejections, *Harper's* magazine published *The Heritage of the Desert* in 1910 and *Riders of the Purple Sage* in 1912. Although the publishing company had been somewhat hesitant to publish *Riders*, it sold over a million copies in a few months.

Before his sudden death from a heart attack in Altadena, California, Grey had written 69 novels and had sold over 25 million copies. Considered more of a story-teller than a literary artist, Grey used much of the same formula in compiling his western romances. Grey spent his last years enjoying his royalties and pursuing his interests as a sportsman in the great out-of-doors of his novels. He was married to Lina Elise Roth. In addition to *Riders of the Purple Sage*, his more popular works include *The Spirit of the Border*, *Desert Gold*, *The Last Trail*, *The Call of the Canyon*, and *The Thundering Herd*.

•GRISHAM, WAYNE R. (1923-) - U.S. representative from California, was born in Lamar, Colorado, and attended the public schools of Long Beach, California, before graduating from Jordan High School in 1940. He graduated from Long Beach City College (A.A. 1947) and Whittier College (B.A. 1949). In 1950 and 1951, he did graduate work at the University of Southern California. During the second World War, he served in the United States Army Air Corps as a fighter pilot in the European theater (1942-1946). Shot down, he was taken as a prisoner of war. Later, he was awarded the Air Medal and the Purple Heart. After the war, he was a teacher and businessman. He was president of the Wayne Grisham Realty and chairman of the borad of directors of

First Mutual Mortgage Company. A La Mirada city councilman from 1970 to 1978, he served two terms as mayor (1973-1974, 1977-1978). Elected to the Ninety-sixth Congress on November 7, 1978, he was reelected two years later. He left office at the end of the Ninety-seventh Congress. He married to Mildred Watt in 1944.

•GROTJAHN, MARTIN, (1904-) - phychiatrist and educator, was born in Berlin, Germany, to Alfred and Charlotte Grotjahn and was educated at Berlin University Medical School where he received his M.D. in 1929. Grotjahn worked at Charite Hospital in Berlin and as head neurological physician at Berlin University from 1933 until 1936, when he came to America. After working at hospitals in the midwest, he was hired in 1946 to teach at the University of Southern California, where he has remained as a clinical professor in the department of psychiatry. He is also an instructor and training analyst at the Southern California Psychoanalytic Institute. Grotjahn in the author of several publications including *Beyond Laughter, Psychoanalysis and the Family Neurosis, Pioneers of Psychoanalysis, The Symbol in History and Today.* In 1976, he received the Sigmund Freud award for Psychoanalytic Physicians. He married Etelka Grosz in 1927.

•GUBSER, CHARLES SAMUEL, (1916-) - U. S. representative from California was born in Gilroy, Santa Clara County, California and attended the public schools. He graduated from San Jose State Junior College in 1934, the University of California in 1937 and then took two years of graduate work. He taught at Gilroy Union High School (1939-1943) and was engaged in farming since 1940. A member of the State assembly in 1951 and 1952, he was elected as a Republican to the Eighty-third and to the ten succeeding Congresses and served from 1953 to 1975. Later, he served as chairman of the United States Section of the Canada-United States Permanent Joint Board.

•GWIN, WILLIAM MCKENDRY, (1805-1885) - one of the first two California senators (1850-55, 1857-61), was born in Sumner County, Tennessee. His father was a Methodist preacher. The younger Gwin received a doctorate of medicine in 1828 from Transylvania University, and briefly studied law before moving to Clinton to practice medicine. He was named U.S. Marshall of Hinds County in 1833, and served as a U.S. representative from 1841 to 1843. He moved to California in 1849 and played a major role in the development of the state's constitution and government. Gwin and Gen. John C. Fremont were the first two U.S. senators elected in California (1850). Reelected in 1857, Gwin was a leader of the state's proslavery movement, and an advocate of an independent west coast nation. One of his associates, fellow senator Milton S. Latham, declared in 1860 that California would declare its independence if a civil war broke out. But their plot was unsuccessful, and soon after leaving his senatorial post, Gwin was arrested for disloyalty. Released two years later, he travelled to France, where he obtained the consent of Napolean III for a scheme to attract American colonists to Mexico. But after several unsuccessful years, he abandoned the project and returned to California. He died in New York.

H

•HAGEN, HARLEN FRANCIS, (1914-) - U. S. representative, was born in Lawton, Ramsey County, North Dakota and attended the public schools of Lawton and Long Beach, California. He moved to Long Beach at the age of fifteen and graduated from Long Beach Junior College in 1933, the University of California at Berkeley in 1936, and from the law school of the same university in 1940. Admitted to the bar in 1940, he commenced the practice of law in Hanford, California.

During World War II, he served in the United States Army from February 1943 to April 1946 as counterintelligence agent and later, head of the Denver, Colorado office of the Security Intelligence Corps. He holds reserve commission as lieutenant colonel in Army Military Intelligence. A member of the city council of Hanford in 1948 and the state assembly (1949-1952), he was alternate delegate to the Democratic National Convention in 1956 and a delegate in 1960 and 1964. Elected as a Democrat to the Eighty-third and to the six succeeding Congresses (January 3, 1953-January 3, 1967), he was an unsuccessful candidate for reelection in 1966 to the Ninetieth Congress. After leaving office, he resumed the practice of law.

•HAGER, JOHN SHARPENSTEIN, (1818-1890) - U. S. senator, was born in German Valley, Morris County, New Jersey and completed preparatory studies before graduating from Princeton College in 1836. He studied law, was admitted to the bar in 1840 and practiced in Morristown. Moving to California in 1849, he engaged in mining and practiced law in San Francisco.

A member of the State constitutional convention in 1849, he served in the state senate (1852-1854, 1865-1871) and was elected state district judge for the district of San Francisco in 1855, serving six years. He was elected a regent of the University of California in 1871. Elected as an Anti-Monopoly Democrat to the United States Senate to fill the vacancy caused by the resignation of Eugene Casserly, he served from December 23, 1873 to March 3, 1875, but was not a candidate for renomination. A member of the state constitutional convention in 1879, he was also collector of customs of the port of San Francisco (1885-1889). He died in San Francisco.

•HAIGHT, HENRY HUNTLEY, (1825-1878) - tenth governor of California (1868-1872), was born at Rochester, New York and was graduated from Yale college. He studied law and was admitted to the bar at St. Louis, Missouri in October, 1846. Remaining there until 1850, he then found his way to San Francisco and became the United States district court judge for southern California. In 1862 he was appointed United States judge by President Lincoln and in 1867, as the Democratic candidate for governor, he was elected by a majority of 9,546. He served until 1872 when he was defeated in the campaign of 1871 by Newton Booth. He resumed the practice of law. He was a member-elect of the state Constitutional Convention of 1878. He was married to Anna Bissell of Missouri.

During Governor Haight's administration the Central Pacific railroad gave signs of becoming a power in the land, and many persons declared that its directors would decide who should become United States senators--in short, that the state was about to pass under a dangerous monopoly. Accordingly, Governor Haight set himself firmly against the granting of railroad subsidies. In the contest between President Andrew Johnson and the United States Congress, Governor Haight adhered to the president. He also vigorously opposed the increased pay of state legislators and stoutly objected to the fifteenth amendment of the United States Constitution. The California legilature welcomed his lead. It was under his governorship that the legislatiure imposed a penalty of not less than $1,000, nor more than $5,000, or imprisonment, upon anyone bringing to California shores any subject of China or Japan without first presenting evidence of his or her good character to the commissioner of immigration, but the Supreme Court decided against the constitutionality of the statutes. The same year the municipality of San Francisco passed an ordinance forbidding the employment of Chinese on public works of any kind. Haight died in San Francisco September 2, 1878.

•HALLECK, HENRY WAGER, (1815-1872) - soldier and general-in-chief of the federal forces during the Civil War, was born in Westernville, New York. After briefly attended Union College, he ented the United States military academy in 1835. Graduating from there four years later, he was appointed second lieutenant in the army engineering corps and was made an assistant professor. For several years he assisted in the construction of the fortifications in New York Harbor. In 1845, he toured Europe. At the outbreak of the war with Mexico, he was sent to California as engineer of military operations for the Pacific Coast. He took part in several of the major expeditions against Mexico. When the war ended, he was a member of the state's first convention, helping author the constitution. He remained an aide-de-camp to Gen. Bennett Riley until 1854, when he resigned from the army to head a prominent law firm in San Francisco. During the civil war, he was given command of the department of Missouri, which embraced the states of Iowa, Minnesota, Missouri, Wisconsin, Illinois, Arkansas and some of Kentucky. Under his command, the Union troops quickly pushed the Confederates southward. In 1862, he was named commander of the department of Missouri, which stretched from the Alleghany to the Rocky Mountains. That July he was named general-in-chief, effectively becoming commander of all the U.S. forces. When the war ended, and Gen. Ulysses became lieutenant-general of the army, Halleck remained in Washington as chief-of-staff from 1864 to 1865. During the latter year, he became commander of the division of the Pacific, while in 1869, he was moved to Louisville, Kentucky, to head the division of the South. Over the years, he authored several important books and papers, and translated numerous others. He received an LL.D degree from Union College in 1862. He died in Louisville.

•HANNAFORD, MARK WARREN (1925-) - U.S. representative from California, was born in Woodrow, Colorado, and graduated from Anderson High School in Indiana (1943), and Ball State University (B.A. 1950, M.A. 1956). During World War II, he served in the Fifth Air Force Squadron in the Pacific as a technical sergeant. He was an associate professor of political science at Long Beach City College (1966-1974), a Lakewood city councilman (1966-1974), and mayor of Lakewood (1968-1970, 1972-1974). A delegate to the Democratic National Convention in 1968, he was elected as a Democrat to the Ninety-fourth Congress on November 5, 1974. Reelected two years later, he was defeated in a reelection bid in 1978. Since then, he has served as White House coordinator of international trade policy for the United States Commerce Department. He married Sara Jane Lemaster in 1948.

•HAUBIEL, CHARLES, (1892-) - composer and pianist, was born in Delta, Ohio, to Edward Marion Pratt and Mary Matilda Haubiel and graduated from Mannes College of Music in New York City. He also studied in Berlin and Leipzig. He is the composer of the opera *Sunday Costs Five Pesos* (1950) and *The Plane Beyond,* which won the New York Philharmonic Symphony Society Contest in 1938. He also received the Columbia Phonograph Company Award for *Karma: Symphonic Variations,* taking first place in the International Schubert Centennial Contest. In 1977, the Viennese Culture Society presented him with the Johann Award as well. A World War I veteran, he has been a member of the American Society of Composers, the National Association for American Composers and Conductors, and the Bohemians and Musicians Clubs of New York City. He married Mary Rice Storke in 1954.

•HAYAKAWA, SAMUEL ICHIYE (1906-) - U.S. representative from California, was born in Vancouver, Canada, and was educated in the public schools of Calgary and Winnipeg, Canada. He received the following degrees: B.A., English, University of Manitoba (Canada), 1927; M.A., English, McGill University,

Montreal, 1928; Ph.D, English, University of Wisconsin, 1935. Certified in psychology in the state of California in 1959, he became a naturalized United States citizen in 1954. He has been an instructor in English at the University of Wisconsin (1936-1939), an instructor to associate professor English at Illinois Institute of Technology (1939-1947), a lecturer at the University of Chicago (1950-1955), a professor of English at San Francisco State College (1955-1968), and president of San Francisco State (1968-1973). He was appointed president emeritus in 1973. He is the author of *Oliver Wendell Holmes: Selected Poetry and Prose, with Critical Introduction* (1939), *Language in Action* (1941), *Language in Thought and Action* (1949), *Language, Meaning and Maturity* (1954), *The Use and Misuse of Language* (1962), *Funk and Wagnalls' Modern Guide to Synonyms* (1968), and others. He was elected to the United States Senate on November 2, 1976, and served one term. He is married to the former Margedant Peter.

•HICKS, JOHN DONALD, (1890-1972) - historian and educator, was the son of John Kossuth and Harriett Gertrude Wing Hicks and was educated at Northwestern University (B.A. 1913, M.A. 1914) and the Universities of San Francisco and California. He was professor of history at the University of California, Berkeley, from 1942 to 1957, and professor emeritus from 1957 until his death. Before coming to Berkeley, Hicks taught successively at Hauline University, North Carolina College for Women, University of Nebraska, and the University of Wisconsin. Among the books he authored are *The Populist Revolt* (1931), *Republican Ascendancy, 1921-32* (1960), *The Federal Union* (1937), *The American Nation* (1941), *A Short History of American Democracy* (1943), and *My Life With History: an Autobiography* (1968). He married Lucile Harriet Curti in 1921.

•HINSHAW, ANDREW J. (1923-) - U.S. representative from California, was born in Dexter, Missouri, to William A. and Ilene Fleming Hinshaw. Educated in the public schools of Missouri and Los Angeles, he graduated from the University of Southern

California with a B.S. in accounting and economics. He attended also the U.S.C. School of Law and completed an American Institute of REal Estate Appraisers cources there. A veteran of World War II, he served from 1942 to 1945 in the United States Navy, first in Alaska, and then in the Pacific Theater of war aboard troop transports in Iwo Jima, Guam, Okinawa and elsewhere. His public service includes eight years as the asessor of Orange County, California, (1965-1972), ten years with the California State Board of Equalization, and five years with the Los Angeles County Assessor's office. Elected as a Republican to the Ninety-third and Ninety-fourth Congresses, he served until 1977. He is the author of *Analysis of the Assesment Function* (1970), *Management Information System* (1969), *The Assessor and Computerization of Data* (1969), and other writings.

•HOLIFIELD, CHET (1903-) - U.S. representative from California, was born in Mayfield, Kentucky, to Ercie V. and Bessie Lee Holifield, and was educated in the public schools of Arkansas. Moving to Montebello, California, in 1920, he was engaged in the manufacturing and selling of men's apparel. A delegate to the Democratic National Conventions in 1940, 1944, 1948, 1952, 1956, 1960, and 1964, he was elected as a Democrat to the Seventy-eighth Congress in 1942, and was reelected fifteen succeeding times before leaving office in 1974. He was chairman of the Eighty-seventh, Eighty-ninth, and Ninety-first Congresses. He is married to Vernice Caneer.

•HOPKINS, MARK, (1813-1878) - businessman, was born at Henderson, New York, to Mark and Anastasia Lukins Kellog Henderson. His father was a merchant. The family moved to St. Clair, Michigan, in 1825. The young Hopkins left school upon the death of his father in 1828 and after working as a clerk for several years, began studying law at his brother's office in Lockport, New York. Instead of practicing law, he sold plows in New York and Ohio and worked as a bookkeeper in the commission house of James Rowland & Co. in New York City. When gold was discovered in California, he joined with his cousin William K.

Sherwood to form a company of twenty-six men called the New England Trading & Mining Co. With a combined capital of $13,000 invested in a year's stock and equipment, the group sailed to California. Settling in Sacrament, Hopkins began selling supplies to the miners in Placerville. In 1850, he formed a successful partnership with E.H. Miller, Jr., in the grocery business in Sacramento. In 1854, he formed a partnership with Collis P. Huntington in the iron and hardware business in Sacramento. While not aspiring to public office, he took an interest in municipal affairs and served as city councilman. An abolitionist, he allowed the offices of Huntington and Hopkins to used for meetings by the Freesoil men of Sacramento. Almost nightly, a small group of men which included Leland Stanford, Charles and E.B. Crocker and others notable Californians gathered to discuss politics and municipal problems. The necessity for a transcontinental railroad to keep firm the union between the east and west was one of the subjects introduced at these meetings. Theodore D. Judah, a civil engineer, had made surveys for a Sacramento Valley railroad and after applying to the business leaders of San Francisco without success, turned to those of Sacramento. Collis P. Huntington announced that he would be one of eight or ten men to bear the whole expense if Mark Hopkins would consent. Hopkins consented and a group of seven formed to pay the expense of thorough three-year survey. Of those seven, Judah died shortly afterward and one dropped out, leaving Hopkins, Huntington, Standford and the Crocker Brothers, the five who saw the project through to completion. When the railroad company was organized in 1861, Hopkins was made treasurer, a position he held until his death. Over the next few years, Hopkins became a millionaire. After his death in Yuma, Arizona, his relatives fought for his wealth. The subsequent litigation lasted for more than 50 years, one of the longest legal battles in America's history.

•HORNE, CHARLES F., JR., (1906-) - engineer and naval officer, was born in New York City to Charles F. and Sarah Horne and was educated at the United States Naval Academy and Harvard University. A retired Rear Admiral of the United States

Navy, he was formerly the president of the Pomona, California, Division of General Dynamics Corporation and vice president of the General Dynamics Corporation. He stepped down from both positions in 1971 to become a private consultant. He is a member of numerous aeronautic and electronic engineering organizations and has been the recipient of many professional and community awards.

•HOWARD, ARTHUR DAVID, (1906-) - geologist and educator, was born in New York City to Louis and Lena Howard and was educated at New York University (B.S. 1929, M.S. 1931) and Columbia University (Ph.D 1937). He taught geology at New York University from 1932 until 1940. He won the A. Cressey Morrison prize in 1935 from the New York Academy of Sciences, and the Emblem for Meritorious Civilian Service in 1945. He served with the Office of Strategic Services from 1944 to 1946. He was a geologist in Antarctica in 1946-47, and on two occasions, he has been a delegate to the International Geologic Congree. In 1948, he was hired as an associate professor of geology at Stanford University. Three years later, he was promoted to full professor, a post he held until 1971, when became professor emeritus. Later, he was a visiting professor emeritus at North Carolina State University. He has published extensively in his field and belongs to numerous geological organizations. Among the books he has published is the *Geologic History of Middle California,* which appeared in 1979. He married Julia E. Slater in 1937

•HOWARD, DONALD STEVENSON, (1902-) - social worker and educator, was born in Tokyo, Japan, to Alfred and May Stevenson Howard and was educated at Otterbein College (B.A 1925), University of Denver (A.M. 1931), and University of Chicago (Ph.D 1941). After earning his A.M. degree, he worked in a number of social service organizations. Over the years, he was president of the American Association of Social Workers, vice president of the Council on Social Work Education and vice president of the National Conference on Social Welfare. During World War II he served in a civilian capacity in Europe and China with the United Nations Relief, Rehabilitation Administration. Howard published *The WPA and Federal Relief Policy* and contributed to several other books. In 1948, he was hired as professor at University of California, Los Angeles, School of Social Welfare. He married Bernice Norris in 1929.

•**HUNTER, DUNCAN LEE** (1948-) - U.S. representative from California, was born in Riverside, California, and attended Pedley public schools before graduating from Rubidoux High School in 1946. He earned at J.D. from Western State University in 1976. He was a first lieutenant in the United States Army airborne from 1969 to 1971. Admitted to the California bar in 1976, he commenced practice in San Diego. Before becoming a congressman, he was a trial lawyer. On November 4, 1980, he was elected as a Republican to the Ninety-seventh Congress. He was reelected two years later. He married Lynne Layh in 1973.

•**HUNTINGTON, HENRY EDWARDS,** (1850-1927) - capitalist and bibliophile, was born in Oneonta, New York, to Solon and Harriet Huntington. His father was a successful merchant, while his uncle Collis P. Huntington was an early railroad builder. Henry Huntington worked as a hardware store clerk, before his uncle hired him to oversee the sawmill which produced railroad ties for his company. In 1900, his uncle made him superintendent of construction on the Chesapeake, Ohio and Southwestern railroad project. Little by little, as the elder Huntington ammassed his railroad empire, the younger Huntington rose in importance in the company, eventually rising to the position of president of the Southern Pacific. When Collis died in 1900, Henry inherited a vast fortune. He soon began construction of a massive electric railroad system in Los Angeles. Over the next few years, he purchased vast tracts of land in the city, until he became the largest landowner in Southern California. His land holdings multiplied their worth as more and more newcomers began arriving. Among the numerous businesses he either owned or partially owned was the Pacific Light and Power Corp., one of the largest public utility corporations in the nation. In 1910, Huntington built a massive estate in the San Gabriel Valley outside of Los Angeles. It was here that he stored the priceless books he collected. Within his collection, which is considered one of the finest private collections in the world, are such rarities as the Guttenberg Bible, the original folios of Shakespeare, the original manuscript of Benjamin Franklin's autobiography, and many more. Huntington married his uncle's widow.

J

•JACKSON, HELEN HUNT, (1831-1885) - author, was born in Amherst, Massachussetts, to Nathan W. Fiske, a professor of languages and philosophy at Amherst College. She was educated at Ipswich Female Seminary and at the school of Rev. J.S.C. Abbortt. At twenty-one, she married Edward B. Hunt, an engineer in the U.S. Army. Hunt was killed eleven years after their marriage while experimenting with a gun he had invented. The couple's first child had died before he was a year old, while their second child died two years after the death of his father. Jackson's grief was acute. "Lifted Over," her first well-known poem, was written two months after her second child died. "In the White Mountain," her first prose sketch, appeared in the *Independent* in 1866. Over the years she wrote more than 370 articles for that magazine. In 1870, after spending a year in Europe, her first book, *Verses,* was published. She published two books, *Bits of Travel* and *Bits of Talk about Home Matters* in 1873. When her health began failing, she went to Colorado, where she married William Sharpless Jackson, a Colorado Springs banker, in 1875. Over the next five years, she published more than a half dozen books and poems, before turning her attention to the plight of the Indians, focusing in particular on the Poncas tribe. She wrote *Century of Dishonor* in 1881, and sent a copy of it to every member of congress. Soon afterward, she was appointed a special commissioner on the California Mission Indians. During a visit to San Jacinto in 1883, Jackson told a friend that she wanted to write a book detailing the abuse of the Indians, as Harriet Beecher Stowe had done for black slaves in *Uncle Tom's Cabin.* The fruit of her efforts was a book entitled, *Ramona,* the story of Juan Diego, an Indian who was shot to death by a white man for alledgedly stealing a horse. Exhausted from her work, Jackson travelled to Norway for rest, before returning to Colorado, where she was injured in a fall in 1884. The following winter, she was taken to Los Angeles, and then unto San Francisco. She died in San Francisco. Among her many published works were, *Nelly's Silver Mine* (1878), *The Story of Boon* (1879), *Mammy Tittleback's Stories* (1881), *The Training of Children* 1882, and *Sonnets and Lyrics* (1886). Each spring since 1923, the town of San Jacinto has honored Jackson by performing a stage version of *Ramona*.

•JONES, THOMAS AP CATESBY, (1790-1858) - naval officer, was born in Vestmoreland County, Virginia, to Major Catsby and Lettice Corbin Jones. His brother, Roger Jones, was adjutant-general of the United States Army. Thomas entered the navy in 1805, became lieutenant in 1812, commander in 1820, and captain in 1829. He was engaged in suppressing piracy, smuggling, and the slave trade in the Gulf of Mexico from 1808 to 1812. With a small flotilla, he attempted to intercept a British squadron of forty vessels, upon its entrance to lake Borgne in 1814. Although he was wounded and compelled to surrender, his conduct was praised. While commanding a squadron on the Pacific, he took temporary possession of Monterey upon being misinformed that war existed between the United States and Mexico. Because of his error, he was removed from command. Two years later, however, he was incharge of the Pacific Squadron again. In 1850, he was again removed, this time for the unauthorized transportation of several hundred refugees out of Baja California shortly after the end of U.S. war against Mexico. He married Mary W. Carter in 1823, and died in Georgetown, D.C.

•JUDAH, THEODORE DEHONE, (1826-1863) - railroad builder, was born in Bridgeport, Connecticut, to Henry R. Judah, an Episcopal minister. After studying at the Rensselaer Institute, he began working as an engineer for several railroad companies, including the Connecticut Railway, and the Erie Canal. He moved to California in 1854 to become head engineer of the Sacramento Valley Railroad, at a time when many of the nation's railroad building giants were trying to find a way to bring the railroad over the Sierra Nevadas to the Pacific. He surprised the people of

Sacramento by announcing that he had found a long and easy ascent of the Sierra Nevadas by way of Dutch Flat. He called for a series of public meetings on the matter, and at one of them Collis Huntington was present. Arranging for an interview with Judah, Huntington agreed to secure six men who would pledge themselves to pay the expense of a thorough survey across the mountains, which Judah then estimated would cost about $35,000. From this meeting, the Central Pacific Railroad was formed. Along with Judah and Huntington, the other partners in the railroad were Leland Stanford, Charles Crocker, and Mark Hopkins. After surveying and settling on a route near what is now Donner Lake, Judah went to congress asking permission for the undertaking. Once the necessary permission was granted, Judah returned to California to oversee the undertaking. A few years later, however, a rift developed between Judah and the other partners, and he sold out his share. On a trip east a few weeks later, he contracted typhoid fever and died in New York.

K

•**KEARNEY, DENNIS,** (1847-1907) - labor leader, was born in Oakmont, Ireland, and became a sailor when he was only eleven. Settling in San Francisco in 1868, he bought a draying business and soon prospered. After becoming a citizen in 1876, he represented the draymen in the U.S. Senate during a special hearing on their trade grievances. In 1877, Kearney began organizing the "Workingmen's Trade and Labor Union," which was later renamed the "Workingmen's Party of California." The political party was organized to secure the rights of the workers and to overcome the economic inequities prevalent at the time. Kearney, as president of the party, was particularly determined to stop the influx of Chinese immigrants, who were competing against the established residents in the labor market. Arrested several times because of his speeches, he was never convicted. By 1878, the party had grown powerful enough to begin influencing the state politics, yet the power was short lived. During the state constitution convention in 1878, Kearny's party is credited with securing several sundry changes, but by the 1880 presidential election his party had all but collapsed. A few years later, he retired from public life. He married Mary Ann Leary in 1870. He died in Alameda.

•**KEARNEY, STEPHEN WATTS,** (1794-1848) - military governor of California, was born in Newark, New Jersey, to Philip and Susanna Watts Kearny. Kearney studied briefly at Columbia College in 1811, before enlisting in the army as a first lieutenant when the War of 1812 broke out. Over the years, Kearny rose to the rank of major-general while serving predominantly in California and the west. During his early years, he accompanied some of the first major expeditions west, including Capt. Matthew J. Magee's into present-day Minnesota, and Gen. Henry Atkinson's to the headwaters of the Yellowstone. When war broke out with Mexico in 1846, Kearny was ordered to march to California from Santa Fe and take command of the U.S. forces in the west. Arriving in California in early December, General Kearny was met by Lieutenant Archibald Gillespie and a garrison of thirty-five men. On Dec. 6, near the small village of San Pasqual, their forces met a troop of mounted Californians under General Andres Pico. The ensuing battle was one of the bloodiest in the war. Kearny was wounded twice, while eighteen of his men were killed. In an attempt to stave off the attack, three of Kearny's men - Kit Carson, Lieutenant E.F. Beale and an Indian - slipped through the surrounding forces and travelled to San Diego to receive aid from Gen. Robert Stockton. After Stockton arrived, Pico's forces were driven off. A few days later, the California forces surrendered Los Angeles, their key city, and the war came to an end. Commandor Stockton then named Colonel John Fremont California's military governor, while at the same time, the U.S. Government named Kearny as territory leader. When Fremont refused to obey Kearney's orders, he was charged with mutiny and eventually court-martialled. With Fremont gone, Kearney became military governor, serving in that post for three months. Later, Kearney served as governor of Vera Cruz, where he contracted a fatal tropical disease. He died in St. Louis. He married Marry Radford in 1830.

•KELLEY, HALL JACKSON, (1790-1874) - organizer of ill-fated colonization of Oregon, was born in Northword, New Hampshire, to Dr. Benjamin and Mary Gile Kelley, and received his early education in an academy at Gilmanton, where he began teaching school in 1806. In 1813, he graduated from college at Middlebury, Virginia. Five years later, he was placed in control of a Boston school and began writing school texts. When he was dismissed from his job in 1823, he began working as a surveyor and then an engineer. In the late 1820s, he began developing a plan to colonize the Oregon territory. He established the American Society of Encouraging the Settlement of the Oregon Territory, and set a date in 1832 for a departure westward. When the plan was met by contempt in the local press, Kelley began losing his potential colonists. Accompanied by his sole associate, Nathaniel Wyeth, he headed to California, and from there, he set off for the Columbia river. By the time he had arrived at Fort Vancouver in late autumn 1834, he had become very sick. He spent the winter there under the care of the Hudson's Bay Company, before returning east. He soon returned to engineering and spent most of the rest of his life away from the public eye. In 1839, however, he wrote *Memoirs*, a paper on the Oregon Territority. In 1851, he wrote *Letters from an Afflicted Husband to an Astrangled Wife*. He married Mary Baldwin in 1815. She died in 1816. In 1822, he married Mary Perry.

•KETCHUM, WILLIAM M. (1921-1978) - U.S. representative from California, was born in Los Angeles, California, and was educated in a number of Los Angeles schools, incuding the Military School of North Hollywood, where he graduated in 1939. He attended the Colorado School of Mines and the University of Southern California, but left school to enter the armed forces during World War II. He served in the United States Army 77th Infantry Division in the Pacific Theater. In 1950, he was recalled into the service during the Korean conflict and served with the 441st Counterintelligence Corps Detachment in Japan for three years. A cattle rancher and farmer, he was twice president of the San Luis Obispo County Farm Bureau before he was elected in 1966 to the California Assembly, where he remained for six years. He was elected as a Republican to the Ninety-third Congress on November 7, 1972, and was twice reelected. He died in Bakersfield, California, during his campaign for reelection for a fourth term. He was married to Lola Heegaard.

•KING, THOMAS BUTLER, (1800-1864) - statesman, was born in Plamer, Massachussets, to Daniel King, a revolutionary war soldier, and Hannah Lord. When his father died in 1816, Thomas was placed under the care of an uncle, Gen. Zebulon Butler. He attended Westfield Academy, and studied law with Judge Garrick Mallery of Philadelphia. Moving to Georgia in 1823, he marrided Anna Matilda Page, the only daughter of a wealthy plantation owner. King was elected to the state senate in 1832, and the U.S. House of Representatives in 1836. He remained in congress until 1849, when he resigned to explore the new territory of California for Pres. Zachary Taylor. In 1850, he was named collector of the port of San Francisco, which he resigned two years later to return to Georgia. He was again elected a state senator in 1859. Two years later, he accepted an appoinment as state commissioner to organize a line of steamers for direct trade, but the civil war interrupted the mission before it was completed.

•KING, THOMAS STARR, (1824-1864) - clergyman, was born in New York City to a Universalist clegyman. In 1835, his family moved to Charlestown, Massachussets, where Thomas secured a job as a clerk in a dry goods store after his father died. He began teaching school in 1840, and was named principal of West Grammar School in Medford, Massachusset, two years later. At Medford, he began studying for the ministry. After holding charges in various Universalist societies, he moved to Boston, where he headed the Hollis Street Unitarian church, a post he retained for eleven years. It was here that King developed a reputation as a brillant lecturer. In 1850, he was awarded an A.M. from Harvard. A lover of nature, King often spent his summers, and some winters, in the White mountains. In 1853, he began contributing articles about his explorations to the *Boston Transcript.* In 1860, he left Boston to become pastor of a church in San Francisco. His reputation as a brillant lecturer had preceded him to the Pacific Coast, and he was soon invited to address eager audience in California and Oregon. He was also one of the first to call public attention to the beauty of Yosemite. In 1864, shortly after the completion of his new church in San Francisco, he was stricken with a severe attack of diptheria, from which he never recovered. He died in San Francisco.

•KINO, EUSEBIO FRANCISCO, (1645-1711) - Jesuit missionary, was born in Segno, Italy. After joining the Jesuits in 1665, Kino was educated in Freiburg, Germany. For many years, he wanted to be sent as a missionary to China, but his requests were denied, and he was ordered to Mexico instead. He arrived in Mexico City in 1861 during a time when Spain was trying to colonize New Mexico and California. The year after his arrival, Kino was included in Don Isidro De Atondo's expedition to Baja California. The expedition was part of Atondo's scheme to help keep the Spanish pearl fishing industry alive on the east coast of the Gulf of California by placing settlers, soldiers and Jesuit missions along a steady path to California. When the project failed in 1685, Kino returned to Mexico City. In 1867, he again headed north, this time to Pimeria Alta, in Sonora, where he worked with the Pima Indians. In 1701, his missionary work among the Pimas caused him to cross the Colorado River near Yuma and entered Alta California. The crossing marks the beginning of Jesuit missionary work in Alta California. Over the years, he founded numerous missions in both Arizona and California, including ones in Santa Cruz, San Pedro, and San Miguel. A talented cartographer, his maps are credited with dispelling the generally held belief that Baja California was an island. He died at Magalena.

•KREBS, JOHN HANS (1926-) - U.S. representative from California, was born in Berlin, Germany, and was educated in the schools of Tel Aviv, Israel. He graduated from the University of California at Berkeley in 1950 with an A.B. and from Hastings College of Law in 1957 with an LL.B. Admitted to the California bar in 1957, he was a practicing attorney for several years. He served in the United States Army from 1952 to 1954. Later, he was a member of the Fresno County Planning Commission (1965-1969) and Board of Supervisors (1970-1974). He was elected as a Republican to the Ninety-Fourth Congress on November 5, 1974, and was reelected two years later. Defeated in a reelection bid in 1978, he resumed his law practice at the end of the Ninety-fifth Congress.

•KUCHEL, THOMAS HENRY, (1910-) - U.S. senator, was born in Anaheim, California, to Henry and Lutetia Bailey Kuchel. He graduated from the University of Southern California with a bachelor's of arts degree in 1932, and a bachelor's of law in 1935. During the later year, he was admitted into the state bar and began practicing law in his hometown. In 1937, he was elected to the state assembly, serving in that position until 1940. He was elected to the state senate the following year, and served there until 1946. During four of those years, from 1942 to 1945, he served as a lieutenant in the U.S. Naval Reserve during World War II. In 1946, he was named state controller, a post he retained until 1952, when he was appointed to fill a U.S. senate seat which had become vacant with the ascension of Richard Nixon to the vice presidency. Two years later, Kuchel was elected to his first of two consecutive full terms in the senate. He married Betty Mellenthin in 1942.

L

•**LAGOMARSINO, ROBERT J.** (1926-) - U.S. representative from California, was born in Ventura, California, and graduated from the University of California at Santa Barbara (B.A. 1950) and Santa Clara Law School (LL.B 1953). He was admitted to the California bar in 1954 and commenced practice in Ventura. During World War II, he served in the United States Navey from 1944 to 1946. He was elected to the Ojai City Council in 1958 and eight months later was elected mayor, a post he retained fro two terms He was elected to the California Senate by special election in 1961, and was reelected three times. He was the first legislator to receive the Legislative Conservationist of the Year Award by the California and National Wildlife Federation in 1965. Elected as a Republican to the Ninety-third Congress in a special election on March 5, 1974, to fill the vacancy caused by the death of Charles M Teague, he has been reelected to each succeeding Congress, including the current Ninety-eighth. He married Norma Smith in 1960.

LANTOS, THOMAS PETER (1928-) - U.S. representative from California, was born in Budapest, and came to the United State in 1947 an an academic scholarship. He graduated from the University of Washington with a B.A. in 1949 and an M.A. in 1950. He received a Ph.D from the University of California in 1953. During World War II, he was active in the anti-Nazi underground. Over the years, he has been a professor of economics, a consultant, a television news analyst and commentator, a member of the Millbrae Board of Education (1950-1966), an administrative assistant and an economic and foreign policy adviser for the United

States Senate. Elected as a Democrat to the Ninety-seventh Congress on November 4, 1980, he was reelected two years later. He is married to Annette Tillemann.

•LEGGETT, ROBERT L. (1926-) - U.S. representative from California, was born in Vallejo, California, and graduated from the University of California at Berkeley in 1947 with a B.A. in political science, and from Boalt Hall Law School in 1950 with a J.D. After being admitted to the state bar, he became a partner in the law firm of Leggett, Gianola, Dacey and Kramer in Vallejo. During World War II, he served in the United States Navy. Elected to the California Assembly in 1960, he served one term before he was elected to the United States Congress. He was elected as a Democrat to the Eighty-eighth Congress in 1962 and was reelected to each succeeding Congress through the Ninety-sixth. After leaving office, Leggett was hired as a lobbyist for American shipping companies. He is married to Barbara Burnett.

•LEWIS, JERRY (1934-) - U.S. representative from California, attended San Bernardino public schols and graduated from San Bernardino High School (1952). In 1956, he graduated from the University of California at Los Angeles with a B.A. After working as a graduate·intern in public affairs at the Coro Foundation, he was a life insurance underwriter. He was a member of the San Bernardino School Board and served in the California Assembly (1968-1978). Elected to the Ninety-sixth Congress on November 7, 1978, he has been reected twice and is a member of the current Ninety-eighth Congress.

•LLOYD, JAMES F. (1922-) - U.S. representative from California, was born in Helena, Montana, and attended the universities of Oregon and Tulane. He also attended the United States Naval postgraduate school. He graduated from Stanford University in 1958 with a B.A. in political science and from the University of

Southern California in 1966 with an M.A. in political science. He enlisted in the United States Navy in 1942, and served as a fighter pilot in South Pacific after graduating from the naval aviation cadet program. He retired from the military in 1963 as a lieutenant commander. His last duty station was the Navla Base Guantanamo Bay, Cuba, where he acted as Public Information Officer during theBay of Pigs and Cuban Missile Crisis. He was later a manager of public relations for Aerojet General Southern California (1963-1965) He established Lloyd's Public Relations and Avdertising in 1966. Elected to the West Çovina City Council in 1968 and 1972, he was mayor of West Covina in 1973. From 1970 to 1973, he was a political science instructor at Mount San Antonia College in Walnut California. Elected as a Democrat to the Ninety-fourth Congress on November 5, 1974, he was twice reelected. He is married to Jackie Vaughan.

•LORAN, ERLE, (1905-) - artist and educator, was born in Minneapolis, Minnesota, and was educated at the University of Minnesota and the Minneapolis School of Art. A professor emeritus of art at the University of California, Berkeley, he has had his works exhibited at museums and galleries nationwide. He is the author of *Cezanne's Composition* (1942) and he is married to Clyta Sisson.

•LOWERY, WILLIAM DAVID (1947-) - U.S. representative from California, was born in San Diego, California, and attended San Diego public schools, before graduating from Point Loma High School in 1965. He attended San Diego State College from 1965 to 1969. A small businessman, he was a partner of the California Groups and the founder and chairman of the California Concord Group. A member of the San Diego City Council since 1977, he became deputy mayor in 1979 and served until 1980, when he was elected as a Republican to the Ninety-seventh Congress. He was reelected two years later. He married Kathleen Brown in 1968.

•LUNGREN, DANIEL E. (1946-) - U,S. representative from California, was born in Long Beach, California, and graduated from St. Anthony's High School (1964), University of Notre Dame (B.A. cum laude 1968), and Georgetown University Law Center (J.D. 1971). In addition, he studied at the University of Southern California Law Center from 1968 to 1969. After graduating from Georgetown, he was admitted to the California bar in 1972 and commenced practicing law in Long Beach. A staff assistant to former U.S. Senators George Murphy of California and William Brock of Tennessee, he was elected as a Republican to the Ninety-sixth Congress on November 7, 1978. Reelected twice, he is a member of the current Ninety-eighth Congress. He married Barbara Kolls in 1969.

M

•MACBRIDE, THOMAS JAMISON, (1914-) - judge, was born in Sacramento, California, to Frank and Charlotte MacBride and was educated at the University of California, Berkeley, where he received his B.A. Degree. Later, he received an LL.B degree from the Boalt Hall of Law at Berkeley. After passing the bar in 1940, he was named California deputy attorney general in 1941, and remained in that position until 1942. From 1946 to 1961,he was in private practice in Sacramento. He served as a lower U.S. District Court Judge from 1961 until 1967, when he was made chief judge. In 1979, he was promoted to senior judge. During World War II he served as a Combat Intelligencre Officer in the Southwest Pacific. He is married to Martha Harrold.

•MAFFLY, ALFRED EMIL, (1897-) - educator and hospital administrator, was born in San Francisco, California, to Alph and Mathilda Maffly and received a B.S. from the University of California in 1921. Maffly worked in a variety of jobs before joining the Herrick Memorial Hospital in Berkeley as an administrator. From 1933 to 1968, he was the executive director of the hospital. From 1950 to 1972, he was also a lecturer at the School of Public Health at the University of California, while at the same time, he was on the faculty of several other university hospitals. Since 1970 he has been a hospital consultant working under the name of A.E. Maffly Associates. Maffly has been a member of the International Hospital Federation, president of the California Hospital Association and Association of Western Hospitals, vice president of the American College of Hospital Administrators. He served on the Board of Regents of the American College of Hospital Administrators for twelve years, serving from 1958 to 1970. Since 1955, he has also been a member of the House of Delegates of the American Hospital Association. He has authored numerous articles for hospital-related periodicals, and he is on the editorial board of *Hospital Management.* He married Frances H. Henderson in 1924.

•MANN, DELBERT, (1920-) - director and producer, was born in Lawrence, Kansas, to Ora and Delbert Mann and was educated at Vanderbilt University (B.A. 1941) and Yale Drama School (1945-47). He received an M.F.A. from Yale in 1973, and he also holds an honorary LL.B degree from Northland College. Mann served in the United States Air Force as a pilot and squadron intelligence officer and was the recepient of the Distinguished Flying Cross and the Air Medal and Four Clusters. After leaving Yale Drama School, he became distinguished as a director and producer of film, stage and television. In 1955, he received an Academy Award for the direction of *Marty,* which also brought him the Director's Guild Award. Among the television shows he has directed are "Heidi" (1968), "A Man Without a Country" (1973), and "All Quiet on the Western Front." He is married to Ann Caroline Gillespie.

•MARSHALL, JAMES WILSON, (1812-1855) - discoverer of gold that triggered California gold rush, was born in Hope, New Jersey, and worked for a time in his father's business as a wagon builder before immigrating westward. Moving through Indiana and Illinois, he finally settled in Missouri, where he unsuccessfully tried homesteading. He moved to Oregon in 1844, and then to California in 1846, whereupon he secured a position with Gen. John A. Sutter at Sutter's Fort (located in present day Sacramento). He left Sutter briefly to try working his own land, but when the venture failed, he returned to his former employer. In May, 1847, Sutter sent Marshall out to find a potential site for a sawmill. Marshall selected a site at Culmua on the American River, and soon began overseeing the mill's construction. On Monday, January 24, while inspecting the work, he noticed yellow particles mingled with the excavated earth which had been washed by the late rains. He gave it little heed at first, but then began to think it might be gold. During the evening he remarked once or twice quietly, somewhate doubtingly to his coworkers, "Boys, I believe I have found a gold mine." "I reckon not," was the response, "no such luck." The next morning, while again examining the mill, Marshall found a larger piece. On January 28, he took his find to Sutter, who was also unsure of what it was, but after looking through the *American Encyclopedia* their doubts vanished. It was indeed gold and the California Gold Rush was on. Marshall and Sutter tried for a time to mine the river near the mill, but almost overnight, miners began flocking to the river, and crowding the two out. Unsuccessful in sustaining his claim, Marshall became dispaired. Forced, at last, by the influx of miners, he shouldered a pack and spent the last twenty-eight years of his life trampling the mountains and ravines near Culmua, subsisting on rice. Eventually, he received some recognition from the people of California, and was given a small pension. He died in Culmua.

•MASON, RICHARD BARNES, (1797-1850) - soldier, was born in Fairfax County, Virginia. His grandfather was George Mason, an eminent revolutionary stateman and friend of George Washington, Thomas Jefferson, and James Madison. He entered the army in 1817 as a second lieutenant of the infantry. He was made a captain in 1819, a major of the first dragoons in 1833, a lieutenant-colonel in 1836, a colonel in 1846, and a brigadier-general in 1846. He took part in the Black Hawk war, and in 1846-47, he was stationed in California, where he acted as civil and military governor of the state until succeeded by Gen. Bennett Riley. On August 7, 1848, Mason announced the cession of California to the United States, and issued the Laws for the Better Government of California. He died in St. Louis, Missouri.

•MATHIAS, ROBERT B. (1930-) - U.S. representative from California, was born in Tulare, California, and was educated in the public schools before graduating from Tulare High School. He attended Kiski Preparatory School in Saltsburg, Pennsylvania, in 1949, and then received a B.A. degree in education from Stanford University in 1953. He was a captain in the United States Marines from 1954 to 1956. In 1948 and 1952, he represented the United States in the Olympic, winning the Decathlon event both years. From 1949 to 1951, he represented the A.A.U. in Europe. In 1955, he was given a four-month leave from the Marine Corps to join the Department of State for the international promotion of American youth programs. He was the personal representative for President Eisenhower at Melbourne, Australia, Olympics in 1956. Later, he served as a Department of State ambassador to promote participation in educational youth programs in many foreign countries. In 1961, he formed the Bob Mathias Sierra Boys Camp. Elected as a Republican to the Ninetieth Congress, he was reelected three times. After leaving office in 1975, he resumed his work in the Boys Camp. He married Melba Wiser in 1953.

•MATSUI, ROBERT T. (1941) - U.S. representative from California, was born in Sacramento, California, and attended the public schools. He graduated from C.K. McClathy High School in 1959, the University of California at Berkeley in 1963 (A.B.) and Hastings College of Law in 1966 (J.D.). He was admitted to the California bar in 1967 and commenced practicing in Sacramento. A member of the Sacramento City Council from 1971 to 1978, he was vice mayor in 1977. Chairman of Congressman John E. Moss's reelection campaign committee and a member of the California Democratic Central Committee (1973-1978), he was elected as a Democrat to the Ninety-sixth Congress on November 7, 1978. Reelected twice, he is a member of the current Ninety-Eighth Congress. He married Doris K. Okada in 1966.

•MCCLOSKEY, PAUL N., JR. (1927-) - U.S. representative from California, was born in San Bernardino, California, and was educated in the public school of South Pasadena and San Marino. He attended Occidental College and California Institute of Technology under the Navy V-5 Pilot Program. He graduated from Stanford University in 1950 and from the Stanford University Law School in 1953. He served in the United States Navy as a seaman first class from 1945 to 1947. During the Korean conflict, he was a second lieutenant in the United States Marine Corps. A recipient of the Navy Cross, Silver Star and Purple Heart, he was on Active Reserve and Ready Reserve from 1952 to 1967 and retired a colonel. A lecturer at Santa Clara and Stanford Law Schools from 1964 to 1967, he was elected as a Republican to the Ninetieth Congress in a special election on December 12, 1967. He was reelected to each succeeding Congress before leaving office at the end of the Ninety-seventh. He married Caroline Wadsworth in 1949.

•MCFALL, JOHN J. (1918-) - U.S. representative from California, was born in Buffalo, New York, and attended the public schools of Manteca, California. He graduated from Modesto Junion College (1936), the University of California (B.A. 1938) amd Boalt Hall Law School (LL.B. 1941). He was admitted to the California bar in 1941. During World War II, he served as a staff sergeant in the Security Intreeligence Corps from 1942 to 1946. After the war end, he commenced the practice of law in Manteca. He was the mayor of Manteca from 1948 to 1951, and a state assemblyman from 1951 until 1956, when he was elected as a Democrat to the Eighty-fifth Congress. He continued to serve until 1979, when he left office and returned to his law practice after being defeated in a reelection bid the previous year. He is married to Evelyn Anklam.

•MCPHERSON, AIMEE ELIZABETH SEMPLE, (1890-1944) -evangelist, was born in Ontario, Canada, to James Morgan and Minnie Pearce Kennedy. Her father died while she was very young. As an adolescent, she studied for the theatre, but she gave up her dreams to become an actress when she joined the Pentecostal church. In 1908, she married Robert James Semple, a clergyman in the Pentacostal revivalist. Soon afterward, the two set off for China to become missionaries. When Semple died a short time later, McPherson returned to America and began holding revivalist meetings. She moved to Los Angeles in 1918 and quickly established the Angelus Temple, an elaborate structure that housed not only the traditional elements of a chuch, but a radio station as well. Over the years, she developed a massive following. In 1930, she formed the International Church of the Foursquare Gospel, which consisted of hundred of churches across the nation. During the Great Depression, the church is credited with aiding millions of poor people, providing them with food, clothing and shelter. After Semple's death, she married Harold Stewart McPherson in 1913. When that marriage ended in divorce in 1918, she remained single for many years, until marrying David L. Hutton in 1931. She died in Oakland.

•MILLER, GEORGE (1945-) - U.S. representative from California, was born in Richmond, California, and attended the state public schools and Diablo Valley College. He graduated from San Francisco State College in 1968 and from the University of California at Davis School of Law in 1972 (J.D.). He served five years as a legislative aide before he was elected as a Democrat to the Ninety-fourth Congress on November 5, 1974. He has been reelected to each succeeding Congress including the current Ninety-eighth. He is married to Cynthia Caccavo.

•MILLER, GEORGE PAUL (1891-) - U.S. representative from California, was born in San Francisco, California, and graduated from St. Mary's College with the degree of B.S. A veteran of World War I, he served as lieutenant in the field artillery, and was graduated from the School of Fire for Field Artillery at Fort Sill, Oklahoma. He served two terms in the California Assembly (1937-1941) and was the executive secretary to the California Division of Fish and Game (1941-1944). Elected as a Democrat to the Seventy-nineth Congress on November 7, 1944, he was reelected thirteen times before he stepped down from office at the end of the Ninety-second Congress in 1973. In 1967, he received the Robert H. Goddard Memorial Trophy for "his sustained leadership in the formulation and execution of national policy contributing immeasurably to the remarkable accomplishment of the United States space effort." He is married to Esther Perkins.

•MINETA, NORMAN YOSHIO (1931-) - U.S. representative from California, was born in San Jose, California, and attended the state public schools before graduating from the University of California at Berkeley in 1953 with a B.S. in business administration. He served in the United States Army from 1953 to 1956, and was later the owner of Mineta Insurance Agency. A member of the San Jose City Council from 1967 to 1971, he was vice mayor of San Jose from 1968 until 1971 and mayor from 1971 to 1974. He was elected as a Democrat to the Ninety-fourth Congress on November 5, 1974, and has been reelected to each succeeding Congress through the current Ninety-eighth. He married May Hinoki in 1961.

•MOONEY, THOMAS JOSEPH, (1882-1942) - labor leader, was born in Chicago, Illinois, to Bryan and Mary Mooney, and was raised in Holyoke, Massachusetts, after his father died in 1892. By the time he was fourteen, he had dropped out of school and began working in a factory. After becoming apprenticed as an iron molder, he joined the molder's union. He travelled in 1907 to Europe, where he was introduced to socialism. Returning to the United States, he began actively promoting socialism. He moved to San Francisco and was one of the publishers of the *Revolt,* a socialist newspaper. Over the next few years, he became active in numerous radical leftist organizations. In 1916, Mooney, his wife Rena, Warren K. Billings and several others were arrested for alledged complicity in the "preparedness parade" bomb explosion of July 22, 1916, which killed six persons and seriously injured at least twenty-five others. There were few clues in the case, yet the prosecuting attorney, Charles Fickert, was able to to secure the death sentence against Mooney. Yet almost immediately charges were made by labor organizations that the conviction had been obtained by the perjured testimony of a key witness. John B. Densmore, an investigator and solicitor for the U.S. Labor Department, was one of many who supported a retrial. His other supporters included Samuel Gompers of the American Federation of Labor, writer Upton Sinclair, and Fremont Older, the editor of the San Francisco *Chronicle*. Despite the publicity and support, there was never a retrial. Several times the supreme court of California and the Supreme Court of the United States upheld his conviction or refused to intervene. Mooney's sentence was commuted to life imprisonment in 1918, however, and he was released from prison in 1939 when he was pardoned by governor Culbert L. Olson. He died in San Francisco.

•MOORHEAD, CARLOS J. (1922-) - U.S. representative from California, was born in Long Beach, California, and attended Glendale public schools. He graduated from the University of California as Los Angeles (B.A. 1943) and the University of Southern California School of Law (J.D. 1949). He enlisted in the United States Army Researve in June 1942, served three and a half years during World War II, and is presently Judge Advocate with rank of lieutenant colonel. When the war ended, he commenced the practice of law. A member of the State Assembly (1967-1972) and the state Republican Central Committee, he was elected to the Ninety-third Congress on Nobember 7, 1972. He has been reelected to each succeeding Congress, including the current Ninety-eighth. He is married to Valery Joan Tyler.

•MORENO, FRANCIS GARCIA DRIGO S., (late 1700s-1846) -bishop of both Californias, was born in Lagos, Mexico, and graduated from the Seminary of Guadlaxara. Leaving the seminary, he studied theology at the Apostolic College of Our Lady of Guadalupe at Zacatecas, where he entered the Order of St. Francis at the age of seventeen. He was ordained a priest about the year 1824. While at the Franciscan Convent of Our Lady of Guadalupe, he filled the positions of master of novices, bachelor of arts and vicar of the convent. He was appointed prefect of the California missions in 1832 and was given the task of converting the Indians to christianity. Father Gracia arrived in California the following year at a critical period in the missions' existence. Jose Echrandia, the first Mexican governor of California, had recently expelled the missionaries and begun attacking the Indians. Garcia brought new recruits with him and attempted to stave off the impending secularization of the missions. In 1837, the secularization went into affect and the missionaries were denied both civil and religious authority. Garcia personally appealed to the Mexican government, and the order was withdrawn, but the change of policy was too late to restore the missions to their former prosperity. Garcia was elected president of the college at Zacatecas in 1839, and was about to revisit the California missions in 1840, when he received news of his appointment as bishop of both Californias. During his short term as bishop, he actively worked to improve the condition of the Indians. He also founded a seminary at Santa Suex. His health began to fail toward the close of 1845, and he retired to Santa Barbara, where he remained until his death.

•MULFORD, PRENTICE, (1834-1891) - journalist, was born at Sag Harbor, New York. At seventeen, he travelled to San Francisco aboard the clipper *Wizard*, the first of his many nautical adventures. A few years later, he began gold mining in California. Gradually, he began writing. His first article appeared in the *Union Democrat* of Sonora, California, when he was twenty-nine. For nearly three years he wrote for the *Democrat* over the signature of "Dogberry," before accepting a position on the *Golden Era*, the leading weekly literary paper of San Francisco. A year later he left the paper to begin contributing to several journals, among them was the *Dramatic Chronicle*, the seedling from which came the San Francisco *Chronicle*. He briefly edited the Stockton *Gazette* in 1868. In 1872, he travelled to England, where he was engaged as a correspondent for the San Francisco *Bulletin*. He returned to America two years later. Settling in New York, he was named to the editorial staff of the New York *Graphic*. For the next six years, he wrote a column for the

Graphic entitled, "The History of a Day," which chronicled the city's murders, scandals and accidents. He moved to a New Jersey wilderness after leaving the Graphic, and wrote *The Swamp Angel.* Two years after moving to Boston in 1884, he began publishing the *White Cross Library,* a series of books dealing with philosophy and the occult. He continued publishing the series until he died suddenly in Long Island.

N

•NORRIS, FRANK, (1870-1902) - author, was born in Chicago, Illinois, to Benjamin Franklin and Gertrude G. Norris. His father founded a major jewelry house. In 1884, Norris went with his family to San Francisco. He attended a boy's school at Belmont, California, and then studied art at the Julian Academy in Paris for two years. He enrolled in the University of California in 1890. His first book, *Yvernelle,* a three-canto poem of medieval France, was published in 1891. He studied at Harvard University in 1890 and 1895, before he was sent to Johannesburg, South Africa, by the San Francisco *Chronicle,* Chicago *Inter-Ocean,* and *Harper's Weekly.* During the Jameson raid, he rode as a courier for John Hays Hammond and his allies. When the raid failed, he was ordered out of Transvaal by the Boer government. Returning to San Francisco, he contributed to the San Francisco *Wave* in 1896 and 1897. In 1898, Doubleday publishers sent Norris to Cuba as a war correspondent. During that same year, his first novel, *Moran of the Lady Letty,* was published. This was followed by *McTeague* (1899), *Blix* (1899), and *A Man's Woman* (1900). *The Octopus,* the first book in a trilogy, was published in 1901. Unfortunately, Norris died before he could complete the trilogy. The second book, *The Pit,* was published posthumously. The third book was never written. Among the collected works which were published after his death, were *A Deal in White, The Responsibily of the Novelist,* and *The Third Cafe.* Another novel, *Vandover and the Brute,* appeared in 1914. Norris married Jeanette Williamson Black in 1899. He died in San Francisco.

O

•OTIS, HARRISON GRAY, (1837-) - newspaper publisher, was born near Marietta, Ohio, to Stephen and Sarah Dyar Otis. At fourteen, he dropped out of school to become a printer's apprentice. He graduated from Granger's College in Columbus in 1857. While a resident of Louisville, Kentucky, he was sent as a delegate to the Republican national convention at Chicago in 1860 that nominated Lincoln for president. During the civil war, he was an active soldier, rising to the rank of lieutenant-colonel, while fighting in several major battles against the Confederate army. After his discharge, he joined his family at Marietta, where he began publishing a small newspaper. He served in the government printing office in Washington from 1867 to 1870, and was also Washington correspondent of the Ohio *State Journal.* After working in the U.S. Patent Office from 1871 to 1875, he moved to California, and for four years ran the Santa Barbara *Press.* In 1979, he was appointed special agent of the treasury department at Seal Islands, Alaska. In 1882, he purchased a quarter interest of the Los Angeles *Daily Times,* " and was made its publisher. By 1886, he had acquired control of the paper. For almost thirty-five years, Otis remained publisher of the *Times,* watching the publication as it grew into the Times-Mirror Company. During the war with Spain, he served as a brigadier-general over the volunteers. Later he served in the Philippines, where he commanded the major assault at Caloocan. He was brevetted major-general for his "meritorious action" at Caloocan. When the war ended, he resigned his post and returned to publishing. He married Eliza A. Chandler in 1857.

P

•PALOU, FRANCISCO, (c.1722-c.1789) - missionary, was born in Mallorca, Spain. As a young man, he entered the monastery of San Francisco in Palma. He later studied at Palma's Lullian University, where he became a pupil of Junipero Serra, the well-known California missionary. Palou remained at the University until 1749, when he travelled to Mexico with Serra to begin missionary work. For the next nine years, the two worked closely together as missionaries in Sierra Gorda. The two were separated for a time, in 1759, when Serra was called to Mexico City. But within a year, Palau had joined his mentor in the Spanish city, where they would remain until 1767, when they were sent to California. In 1769, Serra was named Father-President of the Baja California missions, and later that year he was sent on the Sacred Expedition with Portola to establish more missions northward. While Serra travelled with Portola, Palou ran the missions in Baja California. When the Franciscan missionaries in Baja were replaced by Dominicans four years later, Palou started northward, hoping to again rendezvous with Serra in Monterey. Along the way, he stopped and set a cross to mark the boundary between Baja and Alta California. The cross was set at a place approximately thirty miles south of the present Mexican border. In 1774, a year after arriving in Monterey, Padou set off to explore the area around San Francisco bay. Two years later, he founded the mission of San Francisco. He remained head of the mission until 1784, when he took over as president of all the Alta California missions upon Serra's death. He moved to Mexico the following year to become head of the College of San Fernando. He died at San Fernando. Over the years, Padou kept an extensive record of Serra and the development of the missions. He wrote extensively of the padre in *Racion Historica de la Vida y Apostolicas Tereas del Venerable Padre Fray Junipero Serra.* In his first history of California, Palou also mentioned Serra. The book was entitled *Noticias de la Nueva California,* finished in 1783, but not published until 1857.

•**PANETTA, LEON EDWARD** (1938-) - U.S. representative from California, was born in Monterey, California, and graduated from Monterey High School in 1956, University of Santa Clara in 1960 with a B.A. degree (magna cum laude), and from the university's law school in 1963 with a J.D. He served as a first lieutenant in the United States Army from 1963 to 1965 and received the Army Commendation Medal. Admitted to the bar in 1965, he commenced practic in Monterey. He was a legislative assistant to United States Senator Thomas H. Kuchel from 1966 to 1969, a special assistant to the Secretary of the Department of Health, Education, and Welfare in 1969, director of the United States Office for Civil Rights from 1969 to 1970, executive assistant to the mayor of New York City from 1970 to 1971, and an attorney for the law firm of Panetta, Thompson and Panetta from 1971 to 1976. A founder of Monterey School of Law, he served as counsel to the Monterey Peninsula Regional Park District from 1972 to 1976. He was elected as a Democrat to the Ninety-fifth Congress on November 2, 1976, and has been reelected to each succeeding Congress. He married Sylvia Marie Varni in 1962. He is also the author of *Bring Us Together* (1971).

•**PASHAYAN, CHARLES, JR.** (1941-) - U.S. representative from California, was born in Fresno, California, and graduated from Bullard High School (1959), Pomona College (B.A. 1963), University of California (J.D. 1968), and Oxford University (B.Litt 1977). He was a captain in the United States Army from 1968 to 1970. He was a Special Assistant to General Counsel of the Department of Health Education, and Welfare from 1973 to 1975. Elected as a Republican to the Ninety-sixth Congress on November 7, 1978, he has been reelected twice and is a member of the current Ninety-eighth Congress.

•**PATTERSON, JERRY MUMFORD** (1934-) - U.S. representative from California, was born in El Paso, Texas, and graduated from Tucson (Arizona) High School, Long Beach State University (B.A. 1960), and the University of California at Los Angeles law school (J.D. 1966). Admitted to the California bar in 1967, he worked as an attorney before being elected to Congress. He served in the United States Coast Guard from 1953 to 1957. He was a Santa Ana city councilman from 1969 until 1973, when he became mayor of the city. Elected as a Democrat to the Ninety-fourth Congress on November 5, 1974, he has been reelected to each succeeding Congress through the current Ninety-eighth Congress.

•**PETTIS, JERRY** (1916-1974) - U.S. representative from California, was born in Phoenix, Arizona. A rancher (citrus-avocado), entreprenuer, airline pilot and flight instructor, he was married to the former Shirley McCumber, the United States congresswoman. During World War II, he was an Air Transport Command pilot in the Pacific Theater. After the war, he was special assistant to the president of United Airlines (1946 to 1950) and the founder of four major companies. From 1948 to 1956, he was a professor of economics at Loma Linda University. He was vice president of the university from 1960 to 1964, when he became chairman of the Board of Councilors. He left the university post in 1967, after having been elected as a Republican to the Ninetieth Congress. Reelected three times, he was killed when the private plane he was piloting crashed near Beaumont, California.

•**PETTIS, SHIRLEY N.,** (1924-) - U.S. representative from California, was born in Mountain View, California, to Harold Oliver and Dorothy Susan O'Neil McCumber. She attended Andrews University in Michigan and the University of California at Berkeley. She operated two major businesses with her husband, Jerry Pettis, the United States congressman. She also managed the family ranch and citrus-avocado grove. Elected as a

Republican to the Ninety-fourth Congress in a special election April 29, 1975, to fill the vacancy caused by the death of her husband, she was reelected to the Ninety-fifth Congress two years later, but lost a reelection bid in 1979. Since leaving office, she has continued to manage her land holdings and business.

•PHELAN, JAMES DUVAL, (1861-19) - senator and mayor of San Francisco, was born in that city to James and Alice Phelan. His father was a leading businessman. The younger Phelan graduated from St. Ignatius College in San Francisco in 1881 and then toured Europe for two years. Returning home, he entered the University of California law school, but failed to earn a degree. In 1890, he began working for his father's recently organized Mutual Savings Bank of San Francisco, serving as president of the company from 1895 to 1921. Over the next several years he was active in numerous civic groups. He founded the Young Men's Democratic League, was appointed vice president of the commission handling the state's participation in the 1893 world's Columbian Exposition, and directed the relief effort in San Francisco following the devastating earthquake of 1906. He was elected mayor of San Francisco for the first of two terms in 1896 as a leading organizer against political corruption. As mayor, he is credited with securing the city's ownership of local public utilities. In 1914, he was elected to the United States Senate. Six years later he was defeated in a reelection bid. He wrote "Travels and Comments" in 1923.

R

•REAGAN, RONALD, (1911-   ), thirty-third governor of California (1967-1975), was born in Tampico, Illinois February 6, 1911. His parents were John Edmond and Nelle (Wilson) Reagan. He married actress Jane Wyman on January 24, 1940. He remarried actress Nancy Davis on March 4, 1952.

Although he is a Republican and a conservative, there is evidence that his early beliefs were left-wing Democratic. As a student at a small college in his native Illinois, he helped lead a strike against budget cuts the college's president had imposed, and was taken off a list of supporters for Helen Gahagan Douglas because his leanings were considered to be too liberal. However, after supporting Eisenhower and Nixon, he changed his registration in 1962.

He was a sports announcer in Iowa for five years before moving to California and the Hollywood film industry. He became a popular movie hero, and then in World War II he served in the Air Force and as president of the Screen Actors' Guild. Later, he became more active in politics and the Republican party, and was elected governor by following a policy laid down by Party central committee chairman Gaylord Parkinson. "Parkinson's Law" can be best described as "Thou shalt not speak ill of any other Republican," and Reagan did much in his campaign to unify party members.

Reagan's first taste of political office was as governor and for two terms, he held a conservative administration concerned with economy, particularly in the areas of higher education, social welfare, and medical aid. In 1976 he ran a close race in the primaries against incumbent President Ford, and in 1980 he has emerged again as a unifier of Republicans for the Presidential nomination, appealing for a return to traditional values and less governmental control.

He won by a large margin over Jimmy Carter and began his term with a celebrity-filled inaugural ball. Although President Reagan claimed he would balance the budget and bring down taxes during his term, the Federal deficit continued to climb at record rates. He had harsh critics among environmentalists, blacks and the unemployed, but he still remained popular despite a severe recession which by 1984 had eased but at the cost of record national budget deficits.

His election campaign in 1984 ranked as one of the most highly polished in U. S. political history and enabled him to defeat Democratic challenger former Vice President Walter Mondale in every State except Mondale's home State of Minnesota and the District of Columbia.

•REES, THOMAS MANKELL, (1925-) - U.S. representative from California, was born in Los Angeles, California and was educated in local public schools. He graduated from Occidental College with a B.A. degree in political science, and later attended University of California.

He served as a combat infantryman with General Patton's Third Army during World War II. He was president of Compania del Pacifico, a Latin American export firm.

A state representative, Fifty-ninth Assembly District (1954-1962) and a state senator (1962-1965), he was also a delegate to Democratic National Conventions of 1956, 1960, 1964, and 1968. Elected as a Democrat to the Eighty-ninth Congress on December 15, 1965, to fill the vacancy caused by the resignation of James Roosevelt, he was reelected to the Ninetieth through the Ninety-Fourth Congresses. He has been practicing law in Washington, D.C., since 1977.

•REINECKE, EDWIN, (1924-) - U.S. representative from California, was born in Medford, Oregon and attended public schools in Beverly Hills, California. He graduated from California Institute of Technology at Pasadena in 1950 with a bachelor of science degree (mechanical engineering).

He enlisted in the United States Navy in November 1942 and was discharged as a radio technician second class in February 1946, while in officers' training.

A professional mechanical engineer in California since 1952, he was president of Febco, Inc., manufacturers of lawn irrigation equipment in 1964.

Elected as a Republican to the Eighty-ninth, Ninetieth, and Ninety-first Congresses, he served from January 3, 1965, until his resignation, January 21, 1969, to become Lieutenant-Governor of California. He was a cnadidate for governor in 1973, but lost the nomination of his party after he had been convicted on a perjury charge related to the Watergate scandal. A year later, a U. S. Court of Appeals overturned the conviction.

After leaving office, Reinecke retired to his ranch outside Sacramento and later opened a restaurant. After selling the restaurant, he entered the real estate business in Cameron Park. In 1983, he was named chairman of the state Republican Party.

•REZANOV, NIKOLAI PETROVICH, (1764-1807) - Russian trader, was born in St. Petersburg. After serving in the Russian army, he joined the civil service. In the late 1790s, he was sent by Czarina Catherine II to Siberia to help Russia expand its empire into America. He helped organize the Russian-American Company, which was formed to colonize Alaska and develop the fur trade along its coast. As the colonies developed, Rezanov began investing ways to improve the flow of supplies to the colonies. He set sail from Kronstadt in 1803 as the leader of an expedition exploring potential sea routes to bring in the needed supplies. After two years of travelling, Rezanov arrived at the Russian trading post in Sitzka, Alaska, in August, 1805. That winter, as the post's supplies dwindled, Rezanov was sent to San Francisco to buy supplies. Don Jose Dario Arguello, the presidio commander, reluctantly agreed to his request only after Rezanov had asked to marry the presidio's daughter. The marriage was to take place after Rezanov brought the supplies back to Sitka. Rezanov, however, never returned to San Francisco. In his notes from the journey, Rezanov recorded that he agreed to the marriage only to secure the supplies. A few years later, on his way home to Russia, he died in Krasnoyarsk.

•RICHARDSON, FRIEND WILLIAM, (1865-1943) _ twenty-fifth governor of California (1922-1927), was born near Ann Arbor, Michigan. His parents were William and Rhoda (Dye) Richardson.

He attended San Bernardino College and then worked as a newspaper publisher in San Bernardino (1896-1901) and in Berkeley (1901-1919). He served as California State Treasurer from 1915 to 1923.

Richardson was elected governor on November 7, 1922 as a Republican, defeating Democrat Thomas Lee Woolwine.

His administration saw intensified opposition to the Progressive wing of the Republican party. The Los Angeles Memorial Coliseum was opened and the Inglewood and Rosecrans oil fields were discovered while Richardson was governor. Also University of California at Los Angeles was dedicated and the harbor at Long Beach had its facilities expanded.

After leaving office on January 4, 1927, he served as publisher of the Alemeda *Times Star* and as California State building and loan commissioner (1932-1933).

He died in Berkeley on September 6, 1943.

•RILEY, BENNETT, (1787-1853) - second territorial governor of California, was born in Alexandria, Virginia. After engaging for a time in clerical work, he enlisted in the army as an ensign of rifles. He was promoted to lieutenant in 1813 following his service in the War of 1812. Over the next several years, he fought in several Indian wars and was raised to the rank of lieutenant colonel. During the 1846-47 war with Mexico, he commanded the second infantry under Gen. Winfield Scott, and later the second brigade under Gen. D.E. Twigg in the campaign against Mexico City. Following the war, he was promoted to major general and was made commander of the department of the Pacific, serving as military governor of California from 1948 until the state's formal government was organized in 1950. He was promoted colonel later that year and commanded the first infantry until he died in Buffalo, New York.

•ROGERS, WILL VANN, JR., (1911-) - U.S. representative from California, was born in New York City, New York, and attended the grade and high schools at Beverly Hills, California. He graduated from Stanford University (B.A., 1935), and was later a newspaper publisher.

He was a second lieutenant in the Field Artillery, Reserve Officers Training Corps (1935-1940). During World War II, he enlisted as a private in the United States Army in June 1942, and was commissioned a second lieutenant of Field Artillery in July 1942. Assigned to the Eight Hundred and Ninety-ninth Tank Destroyer Battalion, he served until December 1942.

Elected as a Democrat to the Seventy-eighth Congress, he served from January 3, 1943, until his resignation May 23, 1944, to return to the United States Army, serving as a lieutenant in the Eight Hundred and Fourteenth Tank Destroyer Battalion until March 1, 1946.

Unsuccessful for election to the United States Senate in 1946, he was a delegate to the Democratic National Conventions in 1948, 1952, and 1956.

He resumed newspaper publishing until 1953. A writer, he was also active in radio and television programs. He was a member of the California State Park Commission (1958-1960) and chairman (1960-1962). Appointed Special Assistant to the Commissioner of Indian Affairs (1967-1969), he was later active in real-estate business in Beverly Hills.

•ROLPH, JAMES, (1869-1934), twenty-seventh governor of California (1930-1934), was born in San Francisco. His parents were James and Margaret (Nicol) Rolph.

He attended Trinity Academy in San Francisco after preliminary public schooling.

He married Annie Marshall Reid June 16, 1900.

James Rolph and Company was a shipping firm established by him and later he was a partner in the insurance firm Rolph, Landis and Ellis.

Nicknamed "Sunny Jim" because of his pleasant personality he was elected mayor of San Francisco in 1911 and served five terms ending in 1930.

Rolph was elected governor on November 4, 1930 as a Republican defeating the Democrat Milton K. Young by a three to one margin. While governor he had to contend with a mass migration from California during the Great Depression. However, after work on the Colorado river Aqueduct was started; a major earthquake struck Long Beach resulting in over $60 million damage. He had continual disagreements with the legislature and generally had difficulty coping with the office of governor. He died while in office on June 2, 1934.

•ROLPH, THOMAS, (1885-1956) - U.S. representative from California, was born in San francisco, California and attended the public schools.

At the age of sixteen, he left Mission High School and started working as an office boy for Williams-Dimond Shipping Co. He later graduated from Humboldt Evening High School.

In 1912, he founded the Rolph-Mills & Co., a building materials sales agency, which he headed until his death.

Elected as a Republican to the Seventy-seventh and Seventy-eighth Congresses (January 3, 1941-January 3, 1945), he was an unsuccessful candidate for reelection in 1944 to the Seventy-ninth Congress. When his second term ended he returned to his building material sales agency. He died in San Francisco.

•ROOSEVELT, JAMES, (1907-) - U.S. Representative from California, was born in New York City, New York, to Eleanor and Franklin D. Roosevelt, the U.S. President.

He attended schools in New York and Washington, D.C., before graduating from Groton School in 1926 and Harvard University, Cambridge, Massachusetts, in 1930.

He began his business career in 1930 as an insurance broker in Boston, Massachusetts. He organized Roosevelt & Sargent, Inc., and served as president until 1937 when he became secretary to President Roosevelt. He worked in the motion-picture industry from November 1938 to November 1940, and then went on active duty as a captain in the United States Marine Corps.

Promoted to colonel April 13, 1944, he served in the Pacific Theater, including the Solomon and Gilbert Islands, the second battle at Midway Island and at Kiska in the Aleutian Islands. Released from active duty in August 1945, he was awarded the Navy Cross and Silver Star.

He rejoined Roosevelt & Sargent, Inc., as executive vice president and established an office in Los Angeles, California, in June 1946. He served as chairman of the board, Roosevelt & Haines, Inc., and as a member of the board of trustees of American Medical Center in Denver, Colorado.

An unsuccessful Democratic candidate for Governor of California in 1950, he was a delegate to the Democratic National Conventions in 1948, 1952, 1956, and 1960. Elected as a Democrat to the Eighty-fourth and to the five succeeding Congresses, he served from January 3, 1955, to September 30, 1965. An unsuccessful candidate for Democratic nomination for mayor of Los Angeles in April 1965, he resigned from Congress effective September 30, 1965, to become United States representative to United Nations Economic and Social Council, a post he resigned in December 1966. Later he was president of Development Company Ltd.

Since 1970, he has worked as a business consultant in Newport Beach, California. In addition, he has served as a trustee of Chapman College in the city of Orange, and he has written three books: *My Parent* (1976), *A Family Matter* (1979) and *Affectionately, F.D.R.* (1959).

•ROSECRANS, WILLIAM STARKE, (1819-1898) - U.S. representative from California, was born in Kingston, Ross County, Ohio.

After completing preparatory studies, he was appointed to the United Stastes Military Academy at West Point in 1838 and graduated in 1842. Brevetted second lieutenant, United States Corps of Engineers, July 1, 1842, he became an assistant professor of engineering at the United States Military Academy (1843-1847). Superintendent of repairs at Fort Adams, Massachusetts, he was in charge of various Government surveys and improvements (1847-1853). Brevetted first lieutenant March 3, 1853, he resigned from the Army April 1, 1854, and engaged as an architect and civil engineer, with residence in Cincinnati.

President of the Coal River Navigation Co., Kanawha County, Virginia (now West Virginia), in 1856, he organized the Preston Coal Oil Co. in 1857 and engaged in the manufacture of kerosene.

During the Civil War, he reentered the service on June 7, 1861, as colonel of the Twenty-third Regiment, Ohio Volunteer Infantry and was commissioned brigadier general, United States Army, May 16, 1861, and later as major general, United States Volunteers, March 21, 1862. By resolution of March 3, 1863, he received the thanks of Congress "for distinguished gallantry and good conduct at the Battle of Murfreesboro, Tennessee." Brevetted major general, United States Army (March 13, 1865, "for gallant and distinguished services at the Battle of Stone River, Tennessee," he was honorable mustered out of Volunteers January 15, 1866. He resigned from the United States Army March 28, 1867, and moved to California, settling in Los Angeles.

He declined the offer of the directorship of the branch mint in 1867 and the Democratic nomination for governor of California, but served as United States Minister to Mexico in 1868 and 1869. He again engaged in civil engineering and was president of the Safety Powder Co., in 1875.

Elected as a Democrat to the Forty-seventh and Forty-eighth Congresses (March 4, 1881-March 3, 1885), he was not a candidate for renomination in 1884. Later he was regent of the State university (1884-1885), and Register of the Treasury (1885-1893). He was reappointed brigadier general on the retired list, United States Army (act of Congress, February 27, 1889), and retired March 1, 1889. He died near Redondo, Los Angeles County, California.

•ROUSSELOT, JOHN HARBIN, (1927-) - U.S. representative from California, was born in Los Angeles, California and attended the public schools of San Marino and South Pasadena. He graduated from Principia College in Elsah, Illinois, in 1949 with an A.B. degree.

A life insurance underwriter (1949-1952), he was assistant public relations director, Pacific Finance Corp. in Los Angeles (1954-1955). He operated a public relations consultant firm there (1954-1958), was director of public information, Federal Housing

Administration, Washington, D.C. (1958-1966), and was deputy to chairman of Board of Equalization, State of California (1956).

A delegate to the republican National Convention in 1956, he was a member of the executive committee, Republican state central committee (1956-1957) and vice chairman, Los Angeles County Republican Central Committee (1956-1958). Elected as a Republican to the Eighty-seventh Congress (January 3, 1961-January 3, 1963), he was an unsuccessful candidate for reelection in 1962 to the Eighty-eighth Congress.

He was a management consultant in the fields of marketing, management systems, and government relations from 1967 to 1970, when he was elected to the Ninety-first Congress in a special election to fill the vacancy caused by the death of Glenard P. Lipscomb. Reelected two years later, he served through the end of the 97th Congress.

•ROYBAL, EDWARD R. (1916-) - U.S. representative from California, was born in Albuquerque, New Mexico, and moved to Los Angeles in 1922. He graduated from Roosevelt High School in 1934 and then joined the Civilian Conservation Corps. He was trained in business administration at the University of California at Los Angeles and at Southwestern University. He served in the United States Army from 1944 to 1945   A social worker and public health educator with the Los Angeles County Tuberculosis and Health Association (1942-1949), he served as a member of the Los Angeles City Council from 1949 until 1962, when he was elected as a Democrat to the Eighty-eighth Congress. He has been reelected to each succeeding Congress, including the current Ninety-eighth. He married Lucille Beserra in 1940

•ROYCE, JOSIAH, (1855-1916) - philosopher, was born at Grass Valley, California, to Josiah and S.E. Bayliss Royce, and attended public school in San Francisco, where his family settled in 1866. At sixteen, he entered the University of California. After graduating in 1875, Royce spent a year at Leipzig and Goettingen. He was then nominated to be among the first twenty fellows for graduate study at Johns Hopkins University. In 1878, he received his Ph.D there, presenting a thesis entitled, *The Interdependence of Human Knowledge.* He spent the next four years teaching English literature at the University of California. The rest of his life was passed at Harvard University, where he went as instructor of philosophy in 1882, became assistant professor in 1885, professor in 1892, and Alford professor of natural religion, moral philosophy and civil polity in 1914. He was Ingersoll lecturer at Harvard in 1899, and Walter Channing Cabot fellow from 1911 to 1914. Along with William James, whom he succeeded, Royce was considered one of Harvard's most eminent philosphers. The problem with which he was most concerned was the relationship between the individual and the community, and between man and the universe. Among his early works were, *California from the Conquest in 1846 to the Second Vigilance Committee,* a history (1886), and *The Feud of Oakfield Creek,* a novel (1887). He gave considerable thought to the plight of black Americans, which was recorded in his papers on *Race Questions, Provincialisms, and Other American Problems* (1908). That same year, he wrote *Philosophy of Love,* probably the clearest expositions of his ideas. He was elected president of the American Psychological Association in 1901 and of the American Philosophical Association in 1903. He was a member of the National Academy of Science and a fellow of the American Academy of Arts and Sciences. He was awarded the honorary degree of LL.D by Aberdeen, Hohns Hopkins, St. Andrews and Yales universities, the Litt.D by Harvard, and the D.Sc by Oxford. In 1880, he married Katharine Head. Among the books he wrote are, *The Religious Aspect of Philosophy* (1885), *The Spirit of Modern Philosophy* (1892), *The Conception of God* (1897), *Studies of Good and Evil* (1898), *The World and the Individual* (1900), *Herbert Spencer* (1904, and *The Problem of Christianity* (1913). He died in Cambridge, Massachussetts.

•**RYAN, LEO J.** (1925-) - U.S. representative from California, was born in Lincoln, Nebraska, and graduated from Creighton University (M.S. 1951). He enlisted in the United States Navy in 1943 and served in submarine service during the second World War. After the war, he was a teacher, school administrator, and member of the South San Francisco Recreation Copmmission. He was later elected to the city council and served as mayor. In 1962, he was elected to the state Assembly. Elected as a Democrat to the Ninety-third Congress on November 7, 1972, he was reelected to the three succeeding terms. He was killed a few days after being reelected to his fourth term in office while he was visiting Guyana investigating a religious cult called the People's Temple, lead by the Reverend Jim Jones. Ryan was the author of *Understanding California Government and Politics.*

S

•SALINGER, PIERRE EMIL GEORGE, (1925- __ U.S. senator from California, was born in San Francisco, California and attended San Francisco State College (1942-1943). He graduated from the University of San Francisco with a B.S., in 1947.

Employed on the editorial staff of the San Francisco Chronicle from July 1942 to July 1943, he resigned to enlist in the United States Navy. He commanded a subchaser in the Pacific Theater of Operations during World War II, was honorable discharged with the rank of lieutenant in July 1946, and was awarded the Navy and Marine Corps Medal for heroic action.

He returned to the editorial staff of the San Francisco Chronicle (1946-1955) and was a lecturer in journalism at Mills College in Oakland (1951-1955).

In 1953, he was appointed secretary to the Democratic legislative caucus in San Francisco and was cofounder of the California Democratic Council in Asilomar. West coast editor and contributing editor of Collier's Magazine in 1955 and 1956, he was also an investigator, Senate Select Committee To Investigate Improper Activities in Labor-Management Relations (1957-1959).

He joined the staff of Senator John F. Kennedy in 1959 and served as his press officer in the 1960 presidential campaign. He was appointed presidential press secretary to President John F. Kennedy on January 20, 1961, and continued in this capacity for President Lyndon B. Johnson until he resigned March 19, 1964, to run for the United States Senate. He won the Democratic nomination in the June 2, 1964, California primary election and was then appointed as a Democrat to the United States Senate to fill the vacancy caused by the death of Clair Engle. He served from August 4, 1964, until his resignation December 31, 1964. He was an unsuccessful candidate in 1964 for election to the full term.

After leaving office, he was vice president of Continental Airlines from 1965 until 1968, when he became president of Gramco Development Company. From 1973 to 1978, he worked as a correspondent for *L'Express*. Hired by the American Broadcasting Corporation as a European correspondent in 1977, he was promoted to bureau chief two years later. In 1981, he wrote *America Held Hostage: The Secret Negotiations* about the Iranian Crisis during the late 1970s.

•SARGENT, AARON AUGUSTUS, (1827-1887) - U.S. senator from California, was born in Newburyport, Essex County, Massachusetts and attended the common schools.

Apprenticed to a cabinetmaker for a short time, he learned the printer's trade and worked for several months in 1847 as a printer in Philadelphia, Pennsylvania. He moved to Washington, D.C., the same year and became secretary to a member of Congress.

He moved to California in 1849 and settled in Nevada City where he was employed on the staff of the *Nevada City Journal*. He later became owner of the paper, studied law, and was admitted to the bar (1854). After commencing practice in Nevada City, he became district attorney for Nevada County in 1855 and 1856, and a member of the state senate in 1856. He resumed the practice of law.

A delegate to the Republican National Convention at Chicago in 1860, he was elected as a Republican to the Thirty-seventh Congress (March 4, 1861-March 3, 1863), but declined to be a candidate for renomination in 1862. Elected to the Forty-first and Forty-second Congresses (March 4, 1869-March 3, 1873), he was not a candidate for renomination in 1872, having become a candidate for United States Senator. Elected to the United States Senate, he served from March 4, 1873, to March 3, 1879, but was not a candidate for reelection.

He engaged in the practice of law in San Francisco (1879-1882), and was later appointed minister to Germany in 1882, served in that capacity until April 1884, when he resigned. He declined to accept the appointment of minister to Russia, returned to California in 1884 and resumed the practice of law. An unsuccessful candidate for the Republican nomination for Senator in 1885, he died in San Francisco.

•SAUND, DALIP SINGH, (1899-1973) - U.S. representative from California, was born in Amritsar, India, and was educated in boarding schools before graduating from University of Punjah (A.B., 1919).

He came to the United States in 1920 to attend the University of California and graduated in 1922 receiving M.A. and Ph.D. degrees.

He became a lettuce farmer in the Imperial Valley of California (1930-1953) and also a distributor of chemical fertilizer in Westmoreland.

He became a citizen of the United States in 1949 and less than a year later was elected judge of Justice Court, Westmoreland Judicial District, county of Imperial, but was denied seat, not having been a citizen one year when elected. He was elected judge of the same court in 1952 and served until his resignation January 1, 1957. A delegate to Democratic National Conventions of 1952, 1956, and 1960. He was elected as a Democrat to the Eighty-fifth, Eighty-sixth, and to the Eighty-seventh Congresses (January 3, 1957-January 3, 1963), but was an unsuccessful candidate for relection in 1962 to the Eighty-eighth Congress.

•SCHMITZ, JOHN GEORGE, (1930-) - U.S. representative from California, was born in Milwaukee, Wisconsin, and graduated from Marquette University High School in 1948. He earned a B.S. degree from Marquette University in 1952 and an M.A. degree from California State College at Long Beach in 1960.

He served as a Marine Corps jet fighter and helicopter pilot from 1952 to 1960, and as a lieutenant colonel, United States Marine Corps Reserve from 1960 to present.

He taught philosophy, history, and political science at Santa Ana College from 1960 to 1970.

Elected as a Republican to the Ninety-first Congress in a special election to fill the vacancy caused by the death of James B. Utt. He was reelected in 1971 and served until 1973. In 1972, he ran unsuccessfully for president as the American Independent Party candidate. He served as a California state senator from 1978 to 1982.

•SCOTT, BYRON NICHOLSON, (1903-) - U.S. representative from California, was born in Council Grove, Morris County, Kansas, and attended the public schools. He graduated from the University of Kansas at Lawrence in 1924, from the University of Southern California at Los Angeles in 1930, and from the National University School of Law in 1949.

He taught school at Tucson, Arizona, from 1924 to 1926, when he moved to Long Beach, California, where he continued to teach until 1934.

A delegate to the California Democratic State conventions 1934-1940 and to the Democratic National Convention at Philadelphia in 1936, he was elected as a Democrat to the Seventy-fourth and Seventy-fifth Congresses (January 3, 1935-January 3, 1939). An unsuccessful candidate for reelection in 1938 to the Seventy-sixth Congress and for election in 1940 to the Seventy-seventh Congress, he was secretary of the California State Highway Commission in 1939 and 1940.

He was engaged in the construction business in 1941 and 1942, and then served with the War Production Board in Washington, D.C. (1942-1945). Admitted to the District of Columbia bar in 1949, he practiced law in Washington, D.C., for many years.

•SCOTT, CHARLES LEWIS, (1827-1899) - U.S. representative from California, was born in Richmond, Henrico County, Virginia, and attended the public schools and Richmond Academy. He graduated from William and Mary College in Williamsburg, Virginia in 1846, studied law, was admitted to the bar in 1847 and commenced practice in Richmond.

He moved to California in 1849, engaged in gold mining, and then resumed the practice of his profession in Sonora in 1851.

A member of the State assembly (1854-1856), he was elected as a Democrat to the Thirty-fifth and Thirty-sixth Congresses (March 4, 1857-March 3, 1861), but was not a candidate for reelection.

During the Civil War, he served as a major in the Fourth Regiment, Alabama Volunteer Infantry, of the Confederate Army and was wounded in the Battle of Bull Run July 21, 1861.

After the war, he engaged in agricultural pursuits in Wilcox County, Alaska, and from 1869 to 1879, he was engaged in journalism.

A delegate to every Democratic National Convention from the end of the Civil War, to 1896, he was appointed by President Cleveland on August 10, 1885, Minister Resident to Venezuela and consul general at Caracas, a position he held until his resignation on March 8, 1889.

He returned to the United States and engaged in agricultural pursuits until his death near Mount Pleasant, Monroe County, Alabama.

•SERRA, JUNIPERO, (1713-1784) - missionary, was sent to Mexico from his native Spain in 1749. Born Miguel Jose Serra on the island of Majorca, he studied and taught philosophy at the Lullian University in Palma, a school emphasizing missionary life. According to Palou, Serra's former pupil and companion to Mexico, the priest often spoke of martyrdom as the true "gold and silver of the Indies." An exercise in self-immolation led him to walk to the capital of Mexico after arriving at Vera Cruz, and on the way he was bitten by a snake or an insect, which lamed him for the rest of his life, remaining swollen and ulcerous. He was a fragile man of 5'2" who drove himself to exhaustion in his missionary work and scourged himself in the Franciscan ideal of mortification of the flesh.

His hard work was rewarded when he was named Father-President of the baja California missions in 1769, and later that year he was sent on the Sacred Expedition with Portola to establish more missions northward. When he arrived at San Diego, he was at first too tired to go on, and stayed there to found the first of nine missions in Alta California with the purpose of converting the Indians. In 1770 he traveled to Monterey with Fages and Costanso to establish a second mission, from which he began other missions. After Fages took the governorship, however, Serra fought with him to gain permission to expand, since Fages claimed there weren't enough soldiers to protect more missions. When Fages was finally transferred to another post after Serra trekked to Mexico City pleading for more support, Serra found he had even more trouble from the new governor, Capt. Fernando Rivera y Moncada, and later governor Felipe de Neve. The problems sprang from the governors' belief that the missions were an arm of the government, and the missionary's belief that the Indians had to be converted to Christianity.

Palou, Serra's friend and follower, wrote of the padre in *Racion Historica de la Vida y Apostolicas Tereas del Venerable Padre Fray Junipero Serra*, published in Mexico City in 1787. In his first history of California, Palou also mentioned Serra; the book was entitled *Noticias de la Nueva California*, finished in 1783, but not published until 1857. Serra's Majorca birthplace was donated to the city of San Francisco in 1932.

•SHANNON, THOMAS BOWLES, (1827-1897) - U.S. representative from California, was born in Westmoreland County, Pennsylvania, and attended the public schools.

He moved to Illinois in 1844 and to California in 1849. He engaged in mercantile pursuits, and was a member of the State assembly in 1859, 1860, and 1862. Elected as a Republican to the Thirty-eighth Congress (March 4, 1863-March 3, 1865), he was not a candidate for renomination in 1864. Appointed surveyor at the port of San Francisco August 11, 1865, he served four years. Again a member of the State assembly in 1871 and 1872, he served as speaker the first year. He was appointed by President Grant as collector of customs at San Francisco and served from July 1, 1872, to August 10. 1880, when he resumed mercantile pursuits. He died in San Francisco.

•SHELLEY, JOHN FRANCIS, (1904-1974) - U.S. representative from California, was born in San Francisco, California, and attended the parochial and public schools. He graduated from the law school of the University of San Francisco in 1932, was admitted to the bar and commenced the practice of law in California. Elected to the state senate in 1938 and reelected in 1942, he served as Democratic labor leader (1938-1946). An unsuccessful Democratic candidate for Lieutenant Governor in 1946, he was president of San Francisco Labor Council from January 1937 to May 1949 and then became secretary. He was elected president of the California American Federation of Labor in 1947, 1948 and 1949, and was a delegate to the Democratic National Conventions in 1940, 1941, 1948, 1952, 1956, and 1960.

He served in temporary service, United States Coast Guard, during World War II on detached duty.

Elected as a Democrat to the Eighty-first Congress to fill the vacancy caused by the death of Richard J. Welch, he was reelected to the Eighty-second and to the six succeeding Congresses and served from November 8, 1949, until his resignation January 7, 1964, to become mayor of San Francisco. He served as mayor until January 8, 1968.

In 1969, he became a legislative advocate for the city of San Francisco in the state legislature.

•SHORTRIDGE, SAMUEL MORGAN, (1861-1943) - U.S. senator from California, was born in Mount Pleasant, Henry County, Iowa, and moved to California with his parents, who settled in San Jose in 1875. He attended the public schools and the Hastings College of Law at San Francisco, California, was admitted to the bar in 1884 and commenced the practice of his profession in San Francisco.

A presidential elector on the Republican ticket in 1888, 1900, and again in 1908, he was elected as a Republican to the United States Senate in 1920. Reelected in 1926, he served from March 4, 1921, to March 3, 1933; an unsuccessful candidate for renomination in 1932, he resumed the practice of law. He was later a special attorney for the Justice Department, Washington, D.C.

•SHUBRICK, WILLIAM BRANFORD, (1790-1874) - naval officer and commander of the Pacific coast, was born on Bull's island, South Carolina. He briefly attended Harvard in 1805 before enlisting as a midshipman in the Navy in 1806. He fought on the Constellation and the Constitution during the war of 1812, was promoted lieutenant in January 1813, and was placed in command of the Levant following its capture in 1815. During the next three years, he sailed around the globe in the Washington, the first U.S. vessel to do so. He was promoted to commander in 1820, and for the next two decades served in a variety of posts on the east coast until being raised to commander of the Pacific Fleet during the war with Mexico. Under his leadership the navy captured Mazatlan, Guaymas, La Paz, San Blas and other ports. In 1853, he was place in command of a the squadron protecting fisheries on the east coast, one of several navy posts he held on that coast until 1858 when he sailed with a fleet to Paraguay on a successful and highly praised mission to seek reparation on the attack of a U.S. vessel. Despite his ties to the south, he refused to join the Confederates during the Civil War. He retired from the navy in 1861, but remained active in some advisory roles. He died in Washington.

•SHUMWAY, NORMAN D. (1934-) - U.S. representative from California, was born in Phoenix, Arizona, and was educated in the public schools of Stockton, California. He graduated from Stockton College in 1954 with an A.A. degree, University of Utah in 1960 with a B.S., and Hastings College of Law in 1963 with an LL.D. Admitted to the California Bar in 1964, he commenced practicing in Downey. Appointed to the San Joaquin County Board of Supervisors by Governor Reagan in 1974, he was reelected later that year and in 1976. In 1978, he was chairman of the board of supervisors. Past chairman of Goodwill Industries of San Joaquin Valley and a member of the board of directors of Goodwill Industries of America, he was a partner in a Stockton law firm and an instructor at San Joaquin Delta College and Humphreys College of Law before he was elected to Congress. He was elected as Republican to the Ninety-sixth Congress on Nobember 7, 1978. Reelected twice, he is a member of the current Ninety-eighth Congress.

•SISK, BERNICE FREDERIC, (1910-) - U.S. Representative from California, was born in Montague, Texas, and at the age of six years moved with his parents to Donley Cgunty, Texas. He attended the Whitefish School and the high school at Abernathy and Meadow, Texas. Later he attended Abilene Christian College (1929-1931). He assisted his father in the operation of a cotton farm, and moving to the San Joaquin Valley of California in 1927, he was employed in a food processing plant until 1941.

During World War II, he served as a civilian flight dispatcher at the Sequoia Air Force training field, Visalia, California, from 1941 to 1945. He was later employed with LeMoss-Smith Tire Co. in Fresno.

Elected as a Democrat to the Eighty-fourth Congress, he served until 1978, when he retired from office.

•SKLAR, GEORGE, (1908-) - novelist and playwright, was born in Meriden, Connecticut, to Ezak and Bertha Sklar and graduated from Yale University with a B.A. in 1929.. He has published numerous novels and plays including *Merry Go Round* (1932), *Parade* (1935), *Life and Death of an American* (1939), and *The Housewarming* (1953). In 1939, he won the John Golden Playwriting Fellowship. A resident of Los Angeles, Sklar is married to Miriam Bleecher.

•SLOAT, JOHN DRAKE, (1780-1867) - naval officer and commander of the Pacific fleet, was born in New York city. Enlisted in the U.S. navy as a midshipman in 1800 but was mustered out the following year upon the passage of the peace establishment act. He again entered the navy as a sailing master in 1812, and served three years on the frigate United States. During the war of that year, he received a silver medal for his gallantry in the capture of the British frigate Macedonian. After a long leave of absence, he served on the schooner Grampus from 1823 to 1825 in a campaign against West Indian pirates. He was made chief commander of the operation in 1824 and was instrumental in the capture of several leading pirates. Following the campaign, he was

promoted master-commandant in 1826, captain in 1837, comman-
dant of the Portsmouth navy yard in 1837, and commander of the
Pacific squadron in 1844. When war looked eminent with Mexico,
Sloat took possession of Monterey. When war started, he oc-
cupied San Francisco and other key California points, before being relieved by Com. Robert F. Stockton. He was placed in command of the Norfolk navy yard in 1847, and retired from active
service four years later. Despite his retirement, he was promoted
commodore in 1862 and rear-admiral in 1866. He died in New
Brighton, New York.

•**SMITH, JEDEDIAH STRONG,** (1798-1831) - fur trader, was
born in Bainbridge, New York, to Jedediah Smith, and began
working as a clerk for a Lake Erie freighter company when he
was thirteen. The next twelve years of his life, as he began to
wander westward, are somewhat sketchy. He accompanied Gen.
William Ashley on his expedition to the west from 1823 to 1826.
When Ashley sold his trading company in the latter year, Smith
was one of three mountain men to buy partial interest in it. During the next four years, Smith became well known as an explorer,
as he headed southwest from the Great Salt Lake into California.
Arriving at Mission San Gabriel on November 27, 1826, he
became the first American to cross overland to California. In
1827, he headed northward towards Oregon. He established a
camp on the American River, and then set out with two others to
explore further. He was forced to abandon the expedition when he
arrived at the Humboldt river, which they were unable to cross.
A few weeks later, he left Salt Lake again for California, but this
time they were attacked by Mohave Indians. All but eight
members of the party were killed. After getting resupplied at the
San Gabriel mission, he headed north. After rejoining the first
party on the American River, he spent that winter in the
Sacramento Valley. In the spring, they headed north again. After
crossing the Umpqua River, the party wa attacked by Umqua Indians, killing everyone but Smith and two of his companions.
Smith, having made his way to the Columbia, remained at Fort
Vancouver until the following spring. In 1831, he headed to Santa
Fe to begin trading in the southwest. Shortly after his arrival, he
was killed near Cimarron by Comanches Indians.

•SMITH, H. ALLEN, (1904-1976) - U.S. representative from California, was born in Dixon, Lee County, Illinois, and attended the public schools. He moved to Los Angeles, California, in 1924 and attended Hollywood High School and the University of California at Los Angeles, before graduating from the University of Southern California (A.B., 1930) and the law school of the same university (LL.B., 1933).

Admitted to the bar in 1934, he practiced law in Los Angeles, until December 1935. He was a special agent for the Federal Bureau of Investigation from December 1935 until August 1942, when he was hired as manager of plant protection, Lockheed Aircraft Corp. He resumed the practice of law in Los Angeles in 1944.

A member of the state assembly (1948-1956), he was a delegate to every State Republican convention since 1948 and a delegate to the Republican National Conventions, 1960 and 1968. He was parliamentarian at 1968 convention. Smith was elected as a Republican to the Eighty-fifth and to the seven succeeding Congresses and served from 1957 until 1973.

•SMITH, SYLVESTER CLARK, (1858-1913) U.S. representative from California, was born near Mount Pleasant, Henry County, Iowa, and attended the district schools and Howe's Academy at Mount Pleasant.

He taught school in Winfield, Iowa; then moved to California in 1879 to engage in agricultural pursuits. He taught school in Colusa and Kern Counties in 1883, studied law and was admitted to the bar in 1885. He commenced practice in Bakersfield, California, where he was employed to edit the Kern County *Echo.*

A member of the State senate (1894-1902), he was an unsuccessful candidate for election in 1902 to the Fifty-eighth Congress. Elected as a Republican to the Fifty-ninth and to the three succeeding Congresses, he served from March 4, 1905, until his death in Los Angeles.

•STANFORD, LELAND, (1824-1893) - eighth governor of California (1862-1864), was born at Watervliet, New York, March 9, 1824.

In his youth Leland Stanford worked on his father's farm,

and assisted in railroad construction work. At the age of twenty he began the study of law and entered the office of Wheaton, Doolittle & Hadley at Albany, New York, in 1845. He was admitted to the New York bar, but in 1848 moved to Port Huron, Wisconsin, where he practiced for four years. The loss of his law library and most of his belongings by fire in 1852 changed his plans for the future, and he decided to go to California, where three of his brothers were engaged in business.

Reaching Sacramento in July, 1852, he proceeded to Michigan Bluff, Placer county, where he opened a general store. In 1856 he became a partner in the business conducted by his brothers in Sacramento, and he moved to that city. This business soon grew to large proportions, mainly due to Leland Stanford's managing ability. He made hosts of friends through his business connections, many of whom urged him to enter the political arena, and in 1857 he was nominated for state treasurer on the Republican ticket.

The Democratic party was in great majority in California before the Civil War, and Leland Stanford, with his party, was defeated. He was again defeated in 1859, when he was Republican candidate for governor. In 1860 he was a delegate to the Republican national convention in Chicago, and after Lincoln's inauguration in 1861 he spent several weeks in Washington conferring with the president and his cabinet about affairs on the Pacific coast. While in Washington the Republicans of California again nominated him for governor of the state, and in the fall of 1861 he was elected California's first Republican governor with a plurality of 33,000 votes. The governor's post during the Civil War was a trying one, for the population of California was about evenly divided in its sympathies between the North and the South. Governor Stanford, however, guided the state through the first two years of the war with such success that both parties, in both branches of the California legislature, voted him the thanks of the people of the state. He not only kept California loyal to the Union, but during his term the state debt was reduced by half, a normal school was authorized, and much important legislation of a local nature was passed.

Prior to his election the Central Pacific Railroad had been projected and he became one of the principal figures in its construction along with Mark Hopkins, C. P. Huntington and Charles Crocker. Crocker supervised the building of the road, Hopkins and Huntington looked after the financing, while Stanford used his influence and legal knowledge to secure the needed legislation. He was president of the company from 1861 until his death. It was he who struck the first blow in the building of the line February 2, 1863, and he drove the last gold spike on May 20, 1869. In 1885 he was elected United States senator on the Republican ticket and was reelected four years later, and was serving in the Senate at the time of his death. He was chairman of a number of important committees, and an earnest advocate of plans to have the national government aid the agricultural classes with loans, or with unencumbered lands during periods of financial depression.

Senator Stanford also founded Leland Stanford Junior University (present day Stanford University), at Palo Alto, California, as a memorial to his only child, Leland Stanford, Jr. He was married September 30, 1850, to Jane Lathrop. She died at Honolulu, enroute for Japan, February 18, 1905, under mysterious circumstances. She was poisoned, but whether accidentally, in taking medicine, or intenionally, by the act of another, was never determined. He died at Palo Alto, June 20, 1893.

•STARK, FORTNEY H., JR. (1931-) - U.S. representative from California, was born in Milwaukee, Wisconsin, and graduated from Wauwatosa (Wisconsin) High School in 1949, Massachusetts Institute of Technology with a B.S. in 1953, and the University of California at Berkeley with an M.B.A. in 1960. He served as a captain in the United States Air Force from 1955 to 1957, and afterwards, became founder and president of the Security National Bank of Walnut Creek, California. A sponsor of the Northern California American Civil Liberties Union and the director of Common Cause (1971-1972), he was elected as a Democrat to the Ninety-third Congress on November 7, 1972. He has been reelected to each succeeding Congress, up through the current Ninety-eighth.

•STARK, FRANKLIN CULVER, (1915-) - attorney, was born in Unityville, South Dakota, to Fred H. and Catherine C. Stark and was educated at Dakota Wesleyan University (A.B. 1937) and Northwestern University School of Law (J.D. 1940). He later received an honorary doctorate from the Dakota university. Since 1947, Stark has been a senior member of the Oakland, California, law firm of Stark, Stewart & Simon. He is a member of the State Bar of California, the Alameda County Bar Association, American Bar Association, American Judicature Society, and a number of civic and philanthropic organizations. During World War Two he served in the United State Navy. He is married to Alice C. Churchill.

•STEINBECK, JOHN ERNST, (1902-1968) - author, has been called California's most important novelist. Born in Salinas, he studied at Stanford University but never completed á degree. While working at odd jobs, he began his literary career with a romantic novel about the pirate-governor of Jamaica, Sir Henry Morgan, entitled *Cup of Gold* (1929). However, he soon turned to the area he knew best--the Salinas Valley in California--for the backdrops of his fiction. *The Pastures of Heaven* was set in a lovely, fictional valley and described middle class morals and conformity in a rural community where no one is at home with the nature surrounding them. In contrast, the farmer protagonist in *To a God Unknown* held a pagan, mystical view of nature. His first great success, *Tortilla Flat*, satirized pretentious values like his earlier work, this time set in Monterey and concerning the carefree *paisanos.* These works, written during the Depression, began to demonstrate Steinbeck's sense of the satirical and tragic, as did *In Dubious Battle* 1936, a novel dealing with migratory farm workers and a self-seeking Communist union organizer. The "battle" between the workers and the growers in the novel was "dubious" in the merits of both sides, and Steinbeck shows contempt for the vigilante supporters of the growers in the book. The story is not completely fiction, however; Steinbeck based it on a similar fight in San Joaquin Valley fields that occurred two years earlier. *Of Mice and Men,* a novelette, also concerned itinerant farmhands.

Steinbeck wrote his greatest work in 1939, *The Grapes of Wrath*. It narrated the experiences of the Joad family, forced to leave their Oklahoma farm in the Dust Bowl, and to move to California. Their lives as migrant workers in the San Joaquin Valley, where children starved in the midst of rotting plenty, came about as a result of Steinbeck's anger at the state's agricultural system. The book was condemned by public school and library systems, but it became a nationwide bestseller and later a Twentieth-Century fox film.

His next novels were of lesser greatness, and included such locales as early Mexico, Norway, and Monterey. His *Cannery Row* was a whimsical narrative in the vein of *Tortilla Flats*, concerning the idle life along Monterey's fishing wharfs.

The next major novel, *East of Eden*, was written in 1952, thirteen years after *The Grapes of Wrath*, and was a family saga spanning nearly a century. Its original title was "Salinas Valley" and was dedicated to his two sons in the hopes that they might learn the history of his maternal ancestors. However, fictional people enter into the book, and the theme of it is reworking of the Cain and Abel story.

In 1962, Steinbeck became the only Californian and one of the few American novelists to win the Nobel Prize for Literature. In the words of the Secretary of the Swedish Academy, "In him, we find the American temperament....

•STEPHENS, WILLIAM DENNISON, (1859-1944) - twenty-fourth governor of California (1917-1922), was born in Eaton, Ohio to Martin F. and Alvina (Leiber) Stephens.

After working briefly on the railroad he moved with his parents to Los Angeles in 1887. He married Flora Rawson in 1891. Within ten years he was a prosperous businessman and a partner in Carr and Stephens' grocery wholesalers and retailers.

Stephens was appointed interim mayor in 1909 after the resignation of Arthur C. Harper. He was elected to Congress in 1910 and served until 1916, first as a Republican then as a Progressive. He was appointed lieutenant-governor when Hiram Johnson was appointed to the United States Senate and thus succeeded him as Governor (March, 1917).

In 1918 Stephens won Progressive, Republican and Prohibition nominations for governor and overwhelmed his opponents in the election. During his regular term he made progress in new highway construction and veteran's welfare programs. He lost the nomination in 1922 and returned to a private law practice in Los Angeles.

His writings are preserved as books titled, *California in the War*, *War Addresses*, and *Patriotic Addresses*.

•STEVENSON, ROBERT LOUIS, (1850-1994) - author, was born in Scotland, but met and fell in love with an Oakland woman when they were both vacationing in France. He followed her back to California in 1879, but she was married and had to wait until her divorce was final in 1880. However, he lived close to her in Monterey, San Francisco and Oakland until they were married. The pair honeymooned with the woman's 12-year-old son on the slope of Mt. St. Helena.   He had been ill for a time, but when he regained health, he and his wife moved back to Scotland and later moved to Switzerland, France, and England in constant search for a better climate for his tuberculosis. They spent a winter in New York, and then rented a yacht from an Oakland doctor to sail to the south seas. Stevenson settled in Samoa, where he spent his last years.

He wrote some fiction dealing with the California locale and history, including *The Wrecker*, written in 1892, which presented a romantic picture of San Francisco. He also described life in Mt. St. Helena in *The Silverado Squatters* (1882). His wife helped him with other California writings, including "The Old Pacific Captiol," and "The New Pacific Capitol," about Monterey and San Francisco respectively. He gathered these and other writings in *From Scotland to Silverado*. A state museum in Monterey commemorates his stay in California with some of his memorabilia. The Silverado Museum in St. Helena features some of his rare books and manuscripts as well.

•**STOCKTON, ROBERT FIELD,** (1795-1866) - U.S. senator (New Jersey), naval officer and commander of the Pacific squadron, was born in Princeton, New Jersey, to Richard Stockton, a United States senator. His grandfather Richard Stockton was a signer of the Declaration of Independence. Stockton briefly attended Princeton college before enlisting in the navy in 1811 as a midshipman aboard the frigate Newport. He served as an aide to the secretary of the navy for a time and then rejoined the frigate in its defence of Baltimore during the War of 1812. He was promoted lieutenant in 1814, and served in the Mediterranean and Lake Erie until 1821 when he was made commander of the warship Alligator on a mission to Africa. It was through this mission that the American colonization society was able to establish the colony of Liberia. He married Harriet M. Potter in 1825, and in 1826, he began a twelve year furlough from the navy. Returning to his hometown, he helped create the Delaware and Raritan canal, and became active in politics. Stockton, promoted to the rank of captain, served as fleet-captain of a Mediterranean squadron in 1838. The next year, he was at home again actively participating in the national election. He turned down an offer as secretary of the navy in 1841. Just before the outbreak of the War with Mexico in 1845, Stockton was given command of the U.S. squadron on the Pacific coast. When war broke out, he seized Los Angeles and appointed Gen. John Fremont as state governor. He captured San Diego soon afterward, and during the second week of 1847, he defeated the Mexican forces at Rio San Gabriel and La Mesa. Later that month, after Mexico ceded California to the United States, Stockton was relieved by Com. William Shubrick and returned home. He resigned from the navy in 1850. In 1851, he was elected to the U.S. senate. He left that post two years later and became president of the Delaware and Raritan canal company, a position he held until his death in Princeton. His son John C. Stockton was also a U.S. Senator. The city of Stockton and Stockton Street in San Francisco were named for him in recognition of his war success.

•STONEMAN, GEORGE, (1822-1894) - fifteenth governor of California (1883-1887), was born at Busti, Chautauqua county, New York, and was educated at Jamestown Academy, and at West Point where he graduated in 1846.

He entered the first dragoons and served in the Mexican war under Captain Philip Kearney. He acted as quartermaster at Santa Fe, and was sent, in 1847, to California with Captain A. J. Smith's command, remaining until 1857 on the Pacific coast, in Oregon, Arizona and California, and becoming aide-de camp to Gen. Wool. In 1855 he became a captain in the twenty-fifth United States Cavalry, and, shortly after, was transferred to Texas, where he was in command of Fort Brown when the Civil War broke out. He served in this conflict with great distinction and on August 16, 1871 he retired from the army as a major general.

Stoneman was elected Governor in 1883 as a Democrat. He encouraged irrigation projects, opposed the political power of the railroads and lowered the state tax rate.

•STORKE, THOMAS MORE, (1876-1971_ - U. S. senator from California was born in Santa Barbara, California, and attended the public schools before graduation from Leland Stanford Junior University, Palo alto, California, with an A.B. in 1898.

He was editor and publisher of Santa Barbara *News-Press* and its predecessors since 1901. A rancher and fruit grower, he served as postmaster of Santa Barbara (1914-1924).

He was a delegate to the Democratic National Conventions in 1924, 1932, and 1936. Appointed as a Democrat to the United States Senate to fill the vacancy caused by the resignation of William Gibbs McAdoo, he served from November 9, 1938, to January 3, 1939, and was not a candidate for election for the full term. when his term ended, he resumed the newspaper business.

Later he was a member of the California Crime Commission (1951-1952) and the board of regents of University of California (1955-1960). He died in Santa Barbara.

•STUBBS, HENRY ELBERT, (1881-1937) - U.S. representative from California, was born in Nampa, Coleman County, Texas, and attended the public schools in Groesbeck, Texas, and Phillips University in Enid, Oklahoma. Ordained a minister of the Christian Church in 1911, he served as pastor of the Christian Church in Frederick, Oklahoma (1911-1914, 1918-1921) and in Kingtisher, Oklahoma (1914-1917). He moved to California in 1921 and served as pastor of the Christian Church in Tulare (1921-1923), and of the Santa Maria Christian Church from 1923 until elected to Congress. Elected as a Democrat to the Seventy-third, Seventy-fourth, and Seventy-fifth Congresses, he served from March 4, 1933, until his death in Washington, D.C.

•SUMNER, CHARLES ALLEN, (1835-1903) - U.S. representative from California, was born in Great Barrington, Massachusetts, and attended Trinity College in Hartford, Connecticut. He studied law, was admitted to the bar and engaged in patent paractice.
He moved to California in 1856 and settled in San Francisco, where he was editor of the *Herald* and *Mirror* in 1861.
During the Civil War, he was appointed in 1862 as captain and assistant quartermaster of United States Volunteers, and served until his resignation in 1864.
He moved to Virginia City, Nevada, and was a member of the state senate (1865-1868) serving as president pro tempore for one session.
He returned to San Francisco in 1868 and became editor of the *Herald.* Elected as a Democrat to the Forty-eighth Congress (March 4, 1883-March 3, 1885), he was an unsuccessful candidate for reelection in 1884 to the Forty-ninth Congress. After leaving office, he resumed the practice of law. He died in San Francisco.

•SUTTER, JOHN AUGUSTUS, (1803-1880) - pioneer, was born in Baden (now Germany) to Swiss parents. He studied at a military college and received a commission in the French army, where he rose to the rank of captain. In 1833, he made plans to lead a group of friends and relatives who wanted to emigrate to America. Setting out before the rest of the party to establish a colony in Missouri, he met disaster when a supply ship, carrying on it all the goods he had ordered with the group's combined capital, sunk. After the accident, he travelled west to New Mexico and onto Fort Vancouver. From there, he sailed to the Sandwich Islands, Honolulu, Sitka and finally to San Francisco. He moved inland to what is now Sacramento and built a stockade, which became known as Sutter's Fort. After establishing a colony there, he was granted a large acreage of land from the Mexican government. By the time California was ceded to the United States, the colony, known as Helvetia, was prospering from farming as a fur trading center, but that was to soon end. On February 2, 1848, one of Sutter's men, James Marshall, discovered gold at Sutter's mill. Within a few weeks the California gold rush had begun. Immigrants began converging on Sutter's land, tearing it up in search of gold, while devouring his livestock to eat. Sutter was reduced to poverty over the next ten years, spending thousands of dollars on legal fees in an unsuccessful attempt to recover his land from squatters. Eventually, he was granted a pension from the California legislature of $250 a month. His homestead was burned in 1864, and in 1873, he moved to Lancaster County, Pennsylvania. He died in Washington, D.C.

•SWING, PHILIP DAVID, (1884-1963) - U.S. Representative from California, was born in San Bernardino, California, and attended the public schools. He graduated from Leland Stanford Junior University in 1905, and was first lieutenant in the California National Guard (1906-1908).

He studied law and was admitted to the bar in 1907. He commenced practice in San Bernardino and served as city attorney of Brawley (1908-1909), deputy district attorney of Imperial County (1908-1911) and district attorney (1911-1915). He was chief counsel of the Imperial Irrigation District (1916-1919) and judge of the superior court of Imperial county (1919-1921).

A delegate to the Republican State conventions at Sacramento (1920-1932), he served as chairman in 1926.

During the First World War he served as a private in the Officers Training Camp at Camp Taylor, Kentucky, in 1918.

He was elected as a Republican to the Sixty-seventh and to the five succeeding Congresses (March 4, 1921-March 3, 1933), but was not a candidate for renomination in 1932.

He resumed law practice, and was appointed a member of the California State Water Resources Board (now California Water Commission) in 1945. Reappointed in 1950, he served until 1958. He died in San Diego.

T

•TALCOTT, BURT LACKLEW, (1920-) U.S. representative from California, was born in Billings, Yellowstone County, Montana, and attended the public schools. He graduated from Leland Stanford University, at Palo Alto, California in 1942 and from Stanford University Law School in 1948. He worked as a journeyman carpenter while attending high school and college.

During World War II, he enlisted in the Army Air Corps in 1942, became a bomber pilot and on a mission over Austria was shot down, wounded, and held for fourteen months in a German prison camp. Discharged in 1945 as a first lieutenant, he was awarded the Air Medal and Purple Heart with clusters.

Admitted to the bar in 1948, he commenced the practice of law the same year in Salinas, California. A member of the County Board of Supervisors from the Salinas-Alisal district (1954-1962), he served as chairman of the board in 1962.

Elected as a Republican to the Eighty-eighth Congress, he served until 1977. Since then, he has been on staff of the American Consulting Engineering Council.

•TEAGUE, CHARLES MCKEVETT, (1909-1974) - U.S. Representative from California, was born in Santa Paula, California, and attended the public schools. He graduated from Stanford University in 1931 and from Stanford Law School in 1934. Admitted to the bar in 1934, he commenced the practice of law in Los Angeles and Ventura.

During World War II, he served in the United States Air Force (1942-1946) and was awarded an Air Force commendation ribbon.

Director of McKevett Corp. and Teague-McKevett Co., he was elected as a Republican to the Eighty-fourth and the eight succeeding Congresses. Reelected in 1974, he died before the Ninety-third Congress ended.

•TEMIANKA, HENRI, (b. ? -) - conductor and violinist, was born in Greeneck, Scotland, and graduated from the Curtis Institute of Music in 1930. He is the founder and conductor of the California Chamber Symphony. Since 1964, he has been a professor of music at California State University, Long Beach. After coming to America in 1940, Temianka served from 1942 to 1944 as senior foreign language editor of the Office of War Information Overseas Branch. Over the years, he has been a guest lecturer at many universities and has made numerous international concert tours. He has produced, written and been the featured performer of many films, as well as author of articles appearing in national and professional magazines. He has recorded for RCA Victor, Decca, Parlophone and Columbia. He has also served as an advisor to the Ford Foundation, Martha Baird Rockefeller Foundation, American String Teacher's Association and the National Federation of Music Clubs. In 1973 he wrote *Facing the Music*. He married Emmy Cowden in 1943.

•TERRY, DAVID S., (1823-1889) - state supreme court justice, was born in Todd County, Kentucky. Sometime in his youth, he moved with his family to Texas, and later fought in the Texas Revolution against Mexico. When the conflict ended, Texas became a state and Terry studied law. He began practicing in Houston, but was soon a soldier again, fighting in the U.S. war against Mexico. He moved to California in 1849 with a group of former Texas Ranger and began mining for gold. As with others who had set out to find riches during the California gold rush, Terry had little success. He moved to Stockton and established a law practice there. As his recognition grew, he became involved in politics. He was elected to the state supreme court in 1855, and two years later became chief justice. During a political power play in 1899 between senators David C. Broderick and William

Gwin, Terry aligned himself with Gwin's proslavery faction. Broderick then called him a "damned miserable wretch," who was as corrupt as the other members of the supreme court. When Terry failed to be renominated, he challenged Broderick to a dual, in which Broderick was killed. Three years later, Terry joined the Confederate army and commanded his own regiment in Texas. When the war ended, he raised cotton briefly in Texas, before returning to his law practice in Stockton. He married Sarah Althea Hill in 1886. At the time, Terry had been defending Hill in a suit against Sen. William Sharon. Hill claimed she was married to Sharon, but he denied it. Sharon died during the middle of the case, and the other two married. Despite Sharon's death, Hill continued her court battle, which was finally decided against her. When she lost an appeal in 1888, she verbally attacked U.S. Supreme Court Justice Stephen Field, who was in charge of the hearing. As Field had her removed from the court for contempt of court, Terry went wild and tried to violently attack him. Both Terry and Hill were jailed for several days. A year later, Terry ran into Field while the latter was dining in a Lathrop, California, hotel. Terry attacked Field and was shot dead by a U.S. marshall who had been assigned to protect the justice.

•THOMAS, WILLIAM M. (1941-) - U.S. representative from California, was born in Wallace, Idaho, and attended the public school in San Pedro and Gardena, California. He graduated from Garden Grove High School (1959), Santa Ana Community College (A.A. 1961), and San Francisco State University (B.A. 1963, M.A. 1965). He was a professor at Bakersfield Community College from 1965 until 1974, when he was elected to the California Assembly. He remained in the Assembly until 1978, when he was elected as a Republican to the Ninety-sixth Congress. Reelected twice, he is a member of the current Ninety-eighth Congress. He married Sharon Lynn Hamilton in 1967.

•THOMPSON, THOMAS LARKIN, (1838-1898) - U.S. representative from California, was born in Charleston, Virginia (now West Virginia), and attended the common schools and Buffalo Academy.

He moved to California in 1855 and settled in Sonoma County, where he established the Petaluma *Journal* the same year. He purchased the Sonoma *Democrat* in 1800, and was the editor of that paper. A delegate to the Democratic National Convention at Cincinnati in 1880 and at Chicago in 1892; he was secretary of the state of California (1882-1886). He declined to be a candidate for renomination. Elected as a Democrat to the Fiftieth Congress (March 4, 1887-March 3, 1889), he was an unsuccessful candidate for reelection in 1888 to the fifty-first Congress.

Appointed on April 4, 1891, as commissioner from California to the World's Fair at Chicago, he was also minister to Brazil from April 24, 1893, to May 17, 1897. He died in Santa Rosa.

•TRAEGER, WILLIAM ISHAM, (1880-1935) - U.S. representative from California was born in Porterville, Tulare County, California, and attended the grammar and high schools of Porterville.

During the Spanish-American War, he served as a private in Company E, First Battalion, California Infantry (later known as Sixth Regiment, California Volunteer Infantry) from May 11 to December 15, 1898.

He graduated from Leland Stanford Junior University in 1901, moved to Los Angeles in 1902 and worked as athletic coach at Ponoma College and later at the University of California. He attended the law department of the University of Southern California at Los Angeles, after serving as a deputy United States marshall (1903-1906) and deputy sheriff of Los Angeles County (1907-1911), he was admitted to the bar in 1909 and commenced the practice of law.

Deputy clerk of the California Supreme Court (1911-1921), and sheriff of Los Angeles County (1921-1932), Traeger was elected as a Republican to the Seventy-third Congress (March 4, 1933-January 3, 1935). An unsuccessful candidate for reelection in 1934 to the Seventy-fourth Congress, he died in Los Angeles a year later.

•TUNNEY, JOHN VARICK (1934-) - U.S. senator and representative from California, was born in New York City, New York, and lived in Stamford, Connecticut for six years, then on a small farm in Amenia, New York, and again in Stamford. The son of a famous boxer, he graduated from Westminster High School in Simsburry, Connecticut, in 1952, Yale University in 1956 (B.A.), and University of Virginia in 1959 (LL.B). In addition, he studied at the Academy of International Law at The Hague, Netherlands, in 1957. Hee was admitted to the bar in Virginia and New York in 1959 and practiced law in New York City until April, 1960, when he joined the United States Air Forced as a judge advocate and was assigned to March Air Force Base. He was discharged as a captain in April, 1963. He taught business law at the Unversity of California in 1961 and 1962. Admitted to the California bar in 1963, he resumed the practice of law in Riverside. He was elected as a Democrat to the Eighty-ninth Congress on November 3, 1964, and was reelected to the two succeeding Congresses before being elected to the United States Senate on November 3, 1977. Since leaving office in 1977, he has practiced law with the Los Angeles firm of Manatt, Phelps, Rothberg and Tunney. He married Kathinka Osborne in 1977.

U

•UTT, JAMES BOYD, (1899-1970) - U.S. representative from California, was born in Tustin, California, and attended the public schools of Orange County. A student at Santa Ana Junior college in 1942 and 1943, he was engaged in agricultural and citrus processing.

He served in the State assembly (1932-1936) and was an inheritance tax appraiser in the State controller's office (1936-1952).

Graduating from the University of Southern California Law School in 1946, he was admitted to the bar in 1947 and commenced the practice of law in Santa Ana.

Elected as a Republican to the Eighty-third and to the eight succeeding Congresses, he served from January 3, 1953, until his death in Bethesda, Maryland.

V

•**VALLEJO, MARIANO GUADALUPE,** (1808-1890) - military commander of California, was the second member of his family in California, and the most well-known. He was commander of the detachment of Monterey's garrison that put down an Indian uprising at Mission San Jose. As a follower of Governor Padres, he opposed the policies and administration of his successor, Gov. Victoria. He married Francisca Benicia Carrillo in 1832, allying two important *Californio* families with their 16 children. He helped defend the Mexican territory against Russian invasion and administered the Solano mission as it became secularized. He was named General, and built up an estate, Casa Grande, facing the new pueblo of Sonoma that he founded. He maintained his vineyards like a feudal baron, using Indian labor, and made Alta California's first wine. The towns of Vallejo and Benicia were later laid out on the site of his estate at Rancho Soscal in Solano County.

A supporter of an independent state of California, Vallejo was named its first military commander, but after conflict with Governor Alvarado over control of the missions, he retreated to his landholdings. As more and more Americans moved into this area, he became amenable to the idea of U.S. annexation. However, even though he hadn't been active as a military officer for years, the group of Americans leading the Bear Flag Revolt invaded his estate in Sonoma and informed him he was a prisoner of war. Vallejo quickly discovered that the invaders weren't sure of what war he was a prisoner of, and after a few glasses of brandy, the commissioners were too befuddled to arrange the capitulation. A teetotaling member of the American brigade finally arrested Vallejo and his brother, but the former Mexican general did not resist, feeling relieved of his country's trust. Not long after, he was released and was elected to join the U.S. constituional convention for the state. In this capacity, he tried to make Benicia (his wife's namesake), the capital, and objected to the bear on the California seal because it rcminded him of the indignities he suffered in the Bear flag Revolt. However, the capital city was finally settled at Sacramento, and Vallejo was assured that the bear symbol on the flag signified no offense to native Californians.

•VAN DEERLIN, LIONEL, (1914-) - U.S. representative from California, was born in Los Angeles, California, and attended the public schools at Oceanside, California. He graduated from the University of Southern California at Los Angeles (B.A., 1937) and studied journalism.

During World War II, he served with the Field Artillery and *Stars and Stripes* newspaper, United States Army, as a staff sergeant from 1944 to 1945, with overseas service in the Mediterranean Theater. He was engaged in work as a newsman (1927-1954), and radio and television news editor and analyst (1952-1961).

A delegate to the Democratic National Convention, in 1964, he was elected as a Democrat to Congress in 1963 for the first of nine consecutive terms.

In 1981 and 1982, he taught at San Diego State University as a lecturer in communications.

•VEYSEY, VICTOR V. (1915-) - U.S. representative from California, was born in Los Angeles, California, and attended Eagle Rock High School. He graduated from California Institute of Technology (B.S. 1936) and Harvard University (M.B.A. 1938). He also did graduate study at Stanford University before becoming a college professor there and at Caltech. Over the years he was a rancher, industrial relations and plant manager for the Developmental Engineering Facility at Caltech, and works manager for General Tire and Rubber Company. He served on

Brawley School District Board, Imperial Valley College Board, and the Advisory Commission for the United States Drug Administration Southwest Irrigation Field Station. He was also district president and state director of the California Beet Growers Association. He served in the California legislature from 1963 to 1971. He was elected as a Republican to the Ninety-second Congress on Nobember 3, 1970. Reelected two years later, he served from 1971 to 1975. In 1983, he was named to California Governor George Deukmejian's cabinet as director of industrial relations.

•VIZCAINO, SEBASTIAN, (c.1550-c.1628) - explorer, is believed to have been born in Corcho, Spain, to Antonio Vizcaino. Much of the information about his early life is sketchy. It is believed his served in Portugal's Royal Army in his late teens. In the 1580s, he sailed to Mexico and Manila, and acquired a large fortune. Over the years, he lead several expeditions into the Gulf of California and along the Pacific Coast. On one of those expeditions in 1602, the first significant maps of the California coast were made. It was on that voyage that Vizcaino discovered Monterey Bay. During the years that followed, Vizcaino lobbied the Spanish government to establish a port in Monterey. Finally, in 1607, it agreed to the port and made Vizcaino its commander. When the viceroy of New Spain objected, however, the plan was dropped. In 1611, Vizcaino then lead an expedition to some legendary, but nonexistent, islands near Japan. He returned to Mexico again in 1614, but little else is known about him.

W

•**WALDIE, JEROME RUSSELL,** (1925-) - U.S. Representative from California, was born in Antioch, California, and attended Antioch public schools. He graduated from University of California in 1950, with degree in political science, and from University of California School of Law (Boalt) in 1953.

   A member of California assembly (1959-1966), he was majority leader of the assembly from 1961 to 1966. Elected as a Democrat by special election to the Eighty-ninth Congress to fill the vacancy caused by the death of John F. Baldwin, he was reelected to the Ninetieth, Ninety-first, and Ninety-second Congresses, serving from 1966 to 1974. During the latter year, he ran unsuccessfully for governor of California. Later, he was appointed chairman of Federal Mines Safety and Health Commission by President Jimmy Carter. In 1981, California Governor Jerry Brown appointed Waldie to the state ALRB post.

•**WALKER, JOSEPH REDDEFORD,** (1798-1876) - pioneer, was born in Nashville, Tennessee. He moved to Calhoun county, Missouri, in 1819, becoming a trapper, and for a time, sheriff. Leaving Missouri to become an explorer, he led Bonneville to the Rocky Mountains in 1832. The following year, he was sent by that officer to explore the country west of Great Salt Lake. Leaving Greek River in July with forty men, Walker followed the Humbolt River towards the coast, discovering on the way the lake and river that were named for him. The Sierras and Indians were almost too much for them, but after much difficulty and close to starving, the small band arrived in California. After a winter in Monterey, they headed east again, this time taking a more southerly route which led them through what is now Walker's

Pass. They rendezvoused with Bonneville at Bear River that June. Although, the officer was displeased the outcome of the mission, Walker had done a lot to increase the geographical knowledge of the west. From then on, most of his life was spent exploring the west and leading emigrants over the Rockies. He lead John Fremont's 1945 expedition over the Rockies. In 1867, Walker moved to Ygnacio Valley in Contra Costa county, California, where he and a nephew lived on a ranch. That is where he died.

•WARREN, EARL, (1891-1974) - U.S. Supreme Court judge and thirtieth governor from California, was born in Los Angeles. His parents were Methias and Crystal (Hernlund) Warren.

His studies were taken at Kern County High School, Bakersfield, California, and at the University of California, Berkeley, where he received his law degrees.

His wife was the former Nina P. Meyers--they were married October 14, 1925.

Warren served in the United States Army during 1917 and 1918 as a second lieutenant.

He engaged in the practice of law in the Bay Area from 1914-1917 and held several State appointed positions and was California Attorney General from 1939 to 1943.

He was elected Governor on November 3, 1942, as a Republican, defeating Governor Culbert Olson, the Democrat. He served an unprecedented three terms. While Warren was Governor the state sales tax was lessened and various social programs enacted including an increase in pension payments for the elderly and unemployment compensation benefits.

Warren was the Republican nominee for Vice President of the United States in 1948 and a Presidential candidate in 1952. In September 1953 he was appointed to the U.S. Supreme Court by President Dwight D. Eisenhower where he served until 1969. He also served as Commission chairman investigating the assassination of President John F. Kennedy. He died in Washington, D.C. on July 9, 1974 after his retirement there.

•WARREN, HENRY, (1894-1981) - composer, was born in Brooklyn, New York. His true name was Salvatore Guaragne. Though he had a high school education, he was mostly self taught. He served in the United States Navy during the First World War, and after the war, he began writing songs for Broadway Musicals. In 1932, he moved to Hollywood, where he began a long association with the film-making industry. Nominated more than fifteen times, he was awarded three Oscars from the Motion Picture Academy for his songs "Lullaby of Broadway," "You'll Never Know," and "On the Atcheson, Topeka and the Santa Fe." The most famous of the more than 300 songs he wrote was probably "42nd Street," but he also penned "Chattanooga Choo-Choo," "You're Getting to Be a Habit with Me," "Shuffle off to Buffalo," "Jeepers Creepers," and "You're My Everything." He wrote for such well-known stars as Fanny Brice, Ed Wynn, Al Jolson, Eddie Cantor, Bing Crosby and Jerry Lewis. He was married to Josephine V. Wensler and he died in Los Angeles.

•WATERMAN, ROBERT WHITNEY, (1826-1891) - seventeenth governor of california (1887-1891), was born at Fairfield, New York. His father was a merchant, who died when Robert was a child. The boy was trained and educated under the care of his brothers at Sycamore, Illinois.

He was clerk in a county store until 1846, when he entered business on his own account at Belvidere, Illinois.

In 1850 he was appointed postmaster at Geneva, Illinois, and the same year went to California, where for about two years he followed mining on Feather River.

In 1854, with Abraham Lincoln, Lyman Turnbull, Owen Lovejoy, Richard Yates, and David Davis, he helped to found the Republican party in Illinois. From 1856 to 1858, he canvassed the state during the Fremont campaign, as well as the United States senatorial contest between Stephen A. Douglas and Abraham Lincoln.

In 1873 he went again to California, settling in San Bernardino in 1874. There he discovered and developed silver mines, in what is known as the "Calceo district" of San Bernardino County. Other mining enterprises of his were highly successful, and he also became an extensive landowner. He took a leading part in the work of developing the railroad system of California, and was chief owner of the Stonewall gold mine in San Diego County, and president of the San Diego, Guyanaca and Eastern Railway.

He was elected lieutenant-governor of California in 1887, and when governor Bartlett died, Waterman succeeded to the governorship, his term expriring January 1, 1891. During his administration irrigation in the state encouragingly progressed under favorable legislation. Bancroft says: "Although not marked by any special features, the administration of Governor Waterman gave general satisfaction to the public, and in his message are many excellent suggestions and remarks." At the expiration of his term he returned to his home in San Bernardino. He died on April 12, 1891.

•WAXMAN, HENRY A. (1939-) - U.S. representative from California, was born in Los Angeles, California, and graduated from the University of California at Los Angles in 1961 with a B.A. degree in political science. He later graduated from the university's law school with a J.D. degree. Admitted to the California bar in 1965, he served three terms as a California assemblyman before he was elected as a Democrat to the Ninety-fourth Congress on November 5, 1974. He has been reelected to each succeeding Congress, including the current Ninety-eighth. He married Janet Kessler in 1971.

•WHITE, CECIL FIELDING, (1900-) - U.S. representative from California, was born in Temple, Bell County, Texas, and attended the public schools of Fort Smith, Arkansas.

He spent most of early youth and boyhood in Fort Smith, but at sixteen years of age, he joined the United States Army and served on the Mexican Border. At the outbreak of the First World War, he went to France as a sergeant in the One Hundred and Forty-second Field Artillery, Thirty-ninth Division (1916-1919).

He worked with the cotton broker firm of George II McFadden as telegrapher, and was later associated with the California Cotton Mills of Oakland, and sent to Fresno as manager of their cotton merchandising department. He founded and operated the Cecil F. White & Co. (1930-1932) and was manager of Cockrell & Co., Little Rock, Arkansas, and Memphis, Tennessee (1933-1935). Also he was manager of Frireson & Co., Memphis, in 1935 and 1936, and vice president and manager of the R. G. Hamilton & Co., Fresno (1936-1944). In 1937, he founded the Pendale Compress & Warehouse Co. at Fresno. He was owner and operator of the Cecil F. White Ranches, Inc., Devils Den, California in 1944.

A delegate to Democratic State Convention in 1948, he was elected as a Democrat to the Eighty-first Congress (January 3, 1949-January 3, 1954), but was an unsuccessful candidate for reelection in 1950 to the Eighty-second Congress. Later engaged in cotton compressing business, he was an unsuccessful candidate for election in 1966 to the Ninetieth Congress.

•WHITE, STEPHEN MALLORY, (1853-1901) - U.S. senator from California, was born in San Francisco, California, and moved with his parents to Santa Cruz County. He attended private and common schools and St. Ignatius College in San Francisco. He graduated from Santa Clara College, in 1871, studied law, was admitted to the bar April 14, 1874, and commenced practice in Los angeles.

District attorney of Los Angeles County in 1882, he was a member of the state senate (1886-1890) and served as president pro tempore both sessions. A member of the board of regents of the University of California, he was a delegate to the Democratic National Conventions in 1888 and 1892. An unsuccessful candidate for election to the United States Senate in 1890, he was elected as a Democrat to the Senate two years later, and served from March 4, 1893, to March 3, 1899. He was a delegate to the Democratic National Convention at Kansas City in 1900, which nominated Bryan and Stevenson. He died in Los Angeles.

•WICKMAN, PAUL EVERETT, (1912-) - businessman, was born in Bisbee, Arizona, to Julius and Hilda Wickman and studied at La Sierra College and Pacific Union College, two small California colleges. From 1944 to 1946 he was the associate secretary for the International Religious Liberty Association. In 1945, he joined the National Lecture Bureau as a Travel Lecturer, a position he retained until 1955, when he was made executive director of the Public Relations Society of America, and also the director of development for the National Society for Crippled Children and Adults, heading the society's Easter Seal Campaign. A member of the Newcomen Society of the American Management Association, he has coauthored a book, *Management in a Rapidly Changing Economy* (1958). He is president of Wickman Pharmaceuticals of Los Angeles.

WIGGINS, CHARLES EDWARD, (1927-) - U.S. representative from California, was born in El Monte, Los Angeles County, California, and attended the public schools.

He served for four and one-half years in the United States Army, Infantry, with thirty-two months overseas during World War II and the Korean War.

A graduate of the University of Southern California with a degree in business administration and finance in 1953, he was also a graduate of the University of Southern California School of law in 1956.

Admitted to the bar, he commenced practice in El Monte, in 1957. A former member and chairman of the El Monte Planning Commission (1954-1960), and a former councilman and mayor of El Monte (1960-1966), he was also a member of the California State Republican Central Committee and the Los Angeles County republican Central Committee. Elected as a Republican to the Ninetieth Congress, he served until 1978. During the Watergate Scandal, he was considered one of President Nixon's strongest supporters. After leaving office, he practiced law in Fullerton, California.

•WIGGINTON, PETER DINWIDDIE, (1839-1890)' - U.S. representative from California, was born in Springfield, Illinois, and moved to Wisconsin with his parents in 1843. After completing preparatory studies, he attended the University of Wisconsin at Madison. He studied law, was admitted to the bar in 1859 and practiced.

Editor of the Dodgeville *Advocate* in Wisconsin, he later moved to Snelling, Merced County, California (1862) and continued the practice of law. District attorney of Merced County (1864-1868), he was elected as a Democrat to the Forty-fourth Congress (March 4, 1875-March 3, 1877). He successfully contested the election of Romualdo Pacheco to the Forty-ninth Congress and served from February 7, 1878, to March 3, 1879.

He settled in San Francisco in 1880 and resumed the practice of law. He was nominated by the American Party as candidate for Vice President in 1888 in place of James R. Geer. He died in Oakland.

•WILLIAMS, ABRAM PEASE, (1832-1911) - U.S. senator from California, was born in New Portland, Somerset county, Maine, and attended the common schools. He completed an academic course at North Anson (Maine) Academy (1846-1848) before attending normal school at Farmington, Maine (1848-1853).

After teaching school at North Anson, he moved to Fairfield, Somerset County, Maine, in 1853 and engaged in mercantile pursuits.

Williams moved to California in 1858 and engaged in mining in Tuolumne County. He resumed mercantile pursuits in 1859, and then moved to San Francisco in 1861 and became an importer, stock raiser, and farmer. One of the founders of the San Francisco Board of Trade and its first president, he was a member of the San Francisco Chamber of Commerce. In addition, he was chairman of the finance committee and treasurer of the republican State committee in 1880, and chairman of the latter committee in 1884.

Elected as a Republican to the United States Senate to fill the vacancy caused by the death of John F. Miller, he served from August 4, 1886, to March 3, 1887, but was not a candidate for renomination in 1887.

Upon leaving office, he resumed the wholesale mercantile business in San Francisco, where he died several years later.

•WILSON, CHARLES HERBERT, (1917-) - U.S. representative from California, was born in Magna, Salt Lake County, Utah, and moved with his parents in 1922 to Los Angeles, California, where he attended the public schools.

He was an employee of a bank from 1935-1942. During World War II, he served as a staff sergeant in the United States Army from June 1942 to December 1945, with oversea service in the European Theater of Operations. In 1945, he established an insurance agency in Los Angeles.

He served in the State legislature (1954-1962) as assemblyman from the Sixty-sixth Assembly District. Elected as a Democrat to the Eighty-eighth Congress, he remained in that post until 1981, when he stepped down from office.

•WILSON, ROBERT CARLTON, (1916-) - U.S. representative from California, was born in Calexico, Imperial County, California, and attended California public schools, San Diego State College, and Otis Art Institute.

During World War II, he operated Conship Commissary and served as a private in the United States Army. He was later made a lieutenant- colonel, United States Marine Corps Reserve.

A partner and vice president of an advertising agency in San Diego, he was chairman of the Republican Congressional.Campaign Committee from 1962 to 1966. elected as a Republican to the Eighty-third Congress in 1953, he remained in office until 1981.

•**WOODS, SAMUAL DAVIS,** (1845-1918) - U.S. represenative from California, was born in Mount Pleasant, Maury County, Tennessee, and moved with his parents to Stockton, California, in February 1850. He attended the public schools, studied law, was admitted to the California bar in April 1875, and practiced law in Stockton and in the city and county of San Francisco.

Elected as a Republican to the Fifty-sixth Congress to fill the vacancy caused by the resignation of Marion De Vries, he was reelected to the Fifty-seventh Congress and served from December 3, 1900, to March 3, 1903. He was not a candidate for reelction in 1902 to the Fifty-eighth Congress.

He resumed the practice of law in San Francisco when his term expired. He died in San Francisco.

•**WOOLFORD, FRANK REARDON,** (1901-) - engineer, was born in Little Rock, Arkansas, and was educated at Harvard University and the Georgia Institute of Technology, where he received his B.S. and C.E. degrees, respectively. He had been employed as an engineer for a few seperate railroad and highway related projects when he was hired by Western Pacific Railroad System Lines in 1948. The following year, the San Francisco company promoted him to Chief Engineer. In 1966, he stepped down from that position to become a private consultant to railroad companies. Over the years, he has been a member of numerous civic and professional organizations. He is married to Kathleen Elizabeth Caldwell.

•**WORKS, JOHN DOWNEY,** (1847-1928) - U.S. senator from California, was born near Rising Sun, Ohio County, Indiana, and attended private schools.

During the Civil War, he served in the Tenth Regiment, Indiana Volunteer Cavalry, of the Union Army.

He studied law, was admitted to the bar in 1868 and commenced practice in Vevay, Indiana.

A member of the Indiana state house of representatives (1878-1880), he moved to San Diego, California, in 1883 and continued the practice of law. He was a judge of the superior court of San Diego County in 1886 and 1887, and associate justice of the supreme court of California, 1888-1891. He moved to Los Angeles in 1896 and was president of the city council in 1910.

Elected as a Republican to the United States Senate, he served from March 4, 1911, to March 3, 1917, but was not a candidate for renomination.

He resumed the practice of law for a short time. He died in Los Angeles.

•WRIGHT, GEORGE WASHINGTON, (1816-1885) - U.S. representative from California, was born in Concord, Massachusetts, and attended the public schools.

Employed in the business department of the Boston *Courier* in 1835 and later engaged in mercantile pursuits in Boston, he moved to California and settled in San Francisco in 1849. Again engaged in mercantile pursuits, he soon became interested in banking and mining. He was one of the founders of the banking house of Palmer, Cook & Co. in San Francisco.

Upon admission of California as a state into the Union Wright was elected as an Independent to the Thirty-first Congress and served from September 11, 1850, to March 3, 1851. He declined to be a candidate for renomination. Affiliated with the Republican Party, he was an ardent supporter of John C. Fremont for President of the United States in 1856.

He moved to Washington, D.C., and toward the close of the Civil War he built, at Buffalo, New York, the *Commodore Perry*, a steam revenue vessel with side screw propellers. After returning to Washington, D.C., he served as attorney of the Choctaw Indians. He declined the portfolio of Secretary of the Interior in the Cabinet of President Johnson.

Retiring from political life he became engaged in private scientific work and was also interested in the prosecution of certain claims pending before Congress. He moved to Dorchester, Massachusetts in 1880 and retired from active pursuits. He died in Dorchester.

•WYNN, WILLIAM JOSEPH, (1860-1935) - U.S. representative from California, was born in San Francisco, California, and attended the public schools.

Apprenticed to the machinist's trade, he subsequently worked in the principal manufacturing establishments of San Francisco. He was a member of the board of supervisors of the city and county of San Francisco from 1902 to 1903, when he was elected by a fusion of the Union Labor and Democratic Parties to the Fifty-eighth Congress. An unsuccessful candidate for reelection in 1904 to the Fifty-ninth Congress, he engaged in the insurance business in San Francisco until his death there.

Y

•YORTY, SAMUEL WILLIAM, (1909-) - U.S. representative from California, was born in Lincoln, Lancaster County, Nebraska, and attended the public schools.

He moved to Los Angeles, California, in 1927, completed prelegal work and studied law at Southwestern University, La Salle University, University of Southern California (1946-1950), and through the extension program at University of California (1918).

Admitted to the bar in 1939, he commenced the practice of law in Los Angeles and was a member of the state assembly from 1936 to 1940.

During World War II, he served as a captain, Combat Intelligence, United States Air Corps, with service in New Guinea and the Philippine Islands (1942-1945).

Again a member of the state assembly in 1949 and 1950, he was elected as a Democrat to the Eighty-second and Eighty-third Congresses (January 3, 1951-January 3, 1955), but was not a candidate for renomination in 1954, when he ran unsuccessfully for election to the United States Senate. Unsuccessful for Democratic nomination as United States Senator in 1956, he resumed the practice of law.

He was elected mayor of Los Angeles in May 1961 for a four-year term, and was reelected in 1965 and 1969. He resumed his law practice in 1973, after stepping down as mayor.

•YOUNG, CLEMENT CALHOUN, (1869-1947), - twenty-sixth governor of California (1926-1931), was born in Lisbon, New Hampshire. His parents were Isaac E. and Mary R. (Calhoun) Young.

He attended San Jose High School, Santa Rosa High School and received his B.L. degree at University of California in 1892.

He was married to Lyla J. Vincent March 15, 1902.

After working as a teacher and later as real estate developer he became a member of the California Assembly and served from 1909-1919.

Richardson served as Lieutenant-Governor (1919-1927) before being elected governor on November 2, 1926 as the Republican candidate. His administration was noted for its efficiency and planning ability. Events during his tenure included the collapse of St. Francis Dam which caused over $30 million in damage and the opening of the Henry Huntington Library and Art Museum in Los Angeles.

Young left office on January 6, 1931, and was then employed by the Mason-McDaffle Company. He died on December 24, 1947 in San Francisco.

•YOUNG, JOHN WELSEY, (1906-) - engineer, was born in Philadelphia, Pennsylvania, to John W. and Mary F. Young and graduated from Drexel Institute in 1928. He worked for a couple different companies before joining North American Aviation in 1930. In 1960, he was promoted to vice president of quality and logistics for the Pacific Palisades firm. In 1970, he was made vice president of operations. He has since retired. Over the years, Young has served as a member of the Visiting Committee of College of Engineering and Science at Drexel Institue of Technology. In addition, he he has been a member of the American Society for Quality Control, American Ordinance Association, and the American Institute of Aeronautics and Astronautics. He married Elizabeth F. Burrows in 1937.

•YOUNG, JOSEPH LOUIS, (1919) - artist, was born in Pittsburgh, Pennsylvania, to Louis and Jennie Young and was educated at Westminster College and the Boston Museum School of Fine Arts. He is considered a pioneer in the integration of art in contemporary architecture, and he has completed over 30 major commissions throughout the country including works for the Los Angeles County Hall of Records, the Los Angeles Police Facilities Building, West Apse of the National Shrine of the Immaculate Conception in Washington, D.C., and the Memorial Gate for Eden Memorial Park in San Fernando, California. Since 1953, he has been director of the Joseph Young Mosaic Workshop. In 1969, he became the founding chairman of the department of architecural arts at Brooks Institute in Santa Barbara. He remained at the institute until 1975. Since 1978, he has headed the visual arts portion of Los Angeles's CETA program. Young is a fellow of the International Institute of Arts and Letters, and is a member of the Shaw Society of Southern California. He is the author of two books on mosaics and has written articles in various newspapers and journals.

•YOUNGER, JESSE ARTHUR, (1893-1967) - U.S. representative from California, was born in Albany, Linn County, Oregon, and moved to Kirkland, Washington, in 1904. He graduated from the University of Washington at Seattle in 1915 and served as graduate manager of athletics until 1917.

During the First World War he was called into Federal service in August 1917 with the Washington National Guard and served overseas for ten months with the Forty-eighth Coast Artillery Corps. Discharged as a captain in June 1919, he served later as vice president, director, and manager of the mortgage loan department of the Seattle Title Trust Co. (1920-1930), president of the Seattle Mortgage Loan Co. (1930-1934), regional appraiser for the Home Owners Loan Corporation, assistant appraiser-adviser for the Home Loan Bank Board, and Chief of the Savings and Loan Division of the Federal Home Loan Bank Board (1934-1937). He moved to San Mateo, California in 1937, and was executive vice president of Citizens Federal Savings & Loan Association in San Francisco (1937-1952).

Elected as a Republican to the Eighty-third and to the seven succeeding Congresses, he served from 1953 until his death in Washington, D.C.